KRIS LINDAHL REAL ESTATE[1] IS EARNING THOUSANDS OF 5-STAR REVIEWS ON GOOGLE AND OTHER MAJOR REVIEW SITES AND CONTINUES TO SCORE AN "A" RATING WITH THE BBB.

"The current economic situation affected our jobs and we could no longer afford to stay in our house. Our house needed work, and once we missed a few payments, we knew we wanted to sell fast and avoid foreclosure. Easy process."

—Steven & Cari

"I inherited a house not too long ago. My plan was to fix up the property myself. Once I started all the repairs, I quickly realized I didn't have the time or resources to take on a project like this. I was able to sell through a *Guaranteed Cash Offer* even though the repairs were half finished."

—Michael

---

[1] "Kris Lindahl Real Estate" and "KLRE" refer to Kris Lindahl Real Estate, LLC.

i

© 2024 Lindahl Realty LLC

"We recently moved my mom into assisted living. I was in charge of getting her house sold. Her house was full of her belongings, needed work, and she also had smoked in it forever. The best way to sell her house fast was through their program. The *Guaranteed Cash Offer* eliminated all of the stress and helped us close quickly so she could get her equity."

—Sharon

"My mom could no longer take care of the upkeep, maintenance and repairs of her house. We wanted to move her to assisted living so she didn't have the stress of trying to take care of a house. She was also a hoarder, and this program allowed us to leave things behind, which helped out so much. The process was quick and easy!"

—Mike

"We were going through a messy divorce and needed to get rid of our house quickly and without every neighbor in our neighborhood knowing our business. I would highly recommend selling with a *Guaranteed Cash Offer* to anyone going through a divorce situation."

—Hillary

"We recently retired and wanted to move into a property that was much smaller and needed less maintenance. The property we sold needed work and it became way too much for us. We tried to start the work and then realized it was too overwhelming for us and we didn't want to take the risk of trying to do it ourselves. The *Guaranteed Cash Offer* was definitely right for our situation."

—Laurie & Tim

"My house was in foreclosure, and the bank was going to take it back within weeks. This program helped me close quickly and avoid foreclosure."

—Tom

"We had a rental property that the tenants didn't take care of. They trashed it as well as smoked in it. We didn't have the funds to take the risk to fix it up. This *Guaranteed Cash Offer* program was an easy way to sell it quickly. We are happy to never have to be landlords again!"

—Jeffrey & Sarah

"I got a job offer and had to relocate right away. My house wasn't ready to sell, and I knew it would take time and needed work. The *Guaranteed Cash Offer* was a great option for my situation."

—Kevin

BE GENEROUS

is our core value at Kris Lindahl Real Estate.
We do our best to live it every day by giving back
to the communities that serve us.

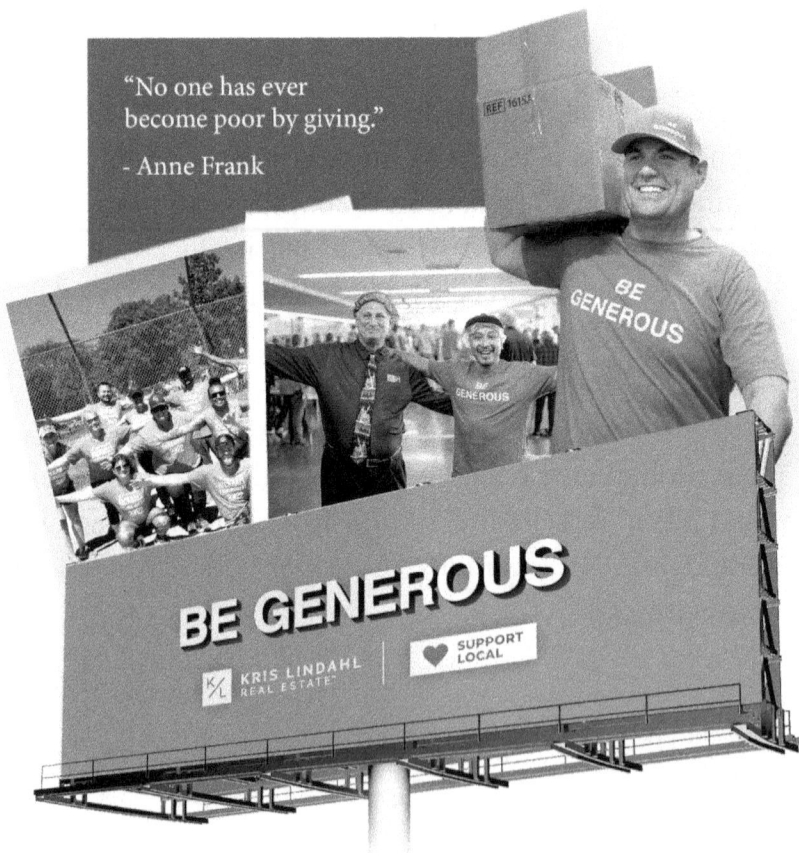

"No one has ever
become poor by giving."

- Anne Frank

BE GENEROUS

KRIS LINDAHL
REAL ESTATE

SUPPORT
LOCAL

Tell us about an organization you're passionate about, whether it's your work organization or business, an organization that has benefited you, or a place you just plain believe in. Let us know why this organization is incredible, and we'll support it.

In the meantime, we encourage you to donate your Time, Talents and Treasures to others in any way possible.

Simply visit
KrisLindahl.com/contact/Kris-Lindahl-Foundation/

vi

GUARANTEED CASH OFFER

ALSO BY KRIS LINDAHL

SOLD!

Expert Advice on
How to Pocket
More Money on Your
Home Sale

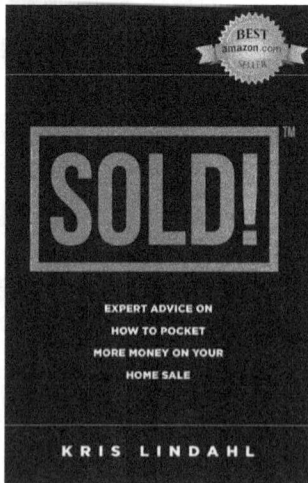

GUARANTEED CASH OFFER

Sell Your Property FAST
With TOTAL CONVENIENCE
And NO COMMISSIONS

CASH NOW, MOVE LATER!

BY **KRIS LINDAHL**

Founder/Owner of Kris Lindahl Real Estate, LLC

V,

As you grow into the remarkable woman you're destined to be, remember that you are the inspiration behind every word I write and every challenge I embrace.

This book is for you, my shining star.

Mama G & Little G,

From the moment you entered our lives, you've changed us for the better and brought us a new energy and brightness. I look forward to the many shared adventures our future holds.

CONTENTS

© 2024 Lindahl Realty LLC

55 SITUATIONS WHERE ACCEPTING A *GUARANTEED CASH OFFER* COULD BE THE SMART THING TO DO.

V. PERSONALITY TRAITS.

© 2024 Lindahl Realty LLC

Note to Readers

THE *GUARANTEED CASH OFFER* PROGRAM is intended to offer the convenience of "no hassle" selling.

When our companies purchase property, we typically complete any renovation, remodeling, repairs or other work we deem appropriate and attempt to resell the property for a profit from which we benefit. The seller from whom we bought the house does not receive any portion of this profit. We do not offer opinions or advice on the fair market value of homes we purchase or the price for which we may resell those homes following any repairs or renovations, nor do we make any promises that our offer will be the highest offer that may be available in the marketplace. Home sales are individual decisions based on individual circumstances. A *Guaranteed Cash Offer* sale is not right for everyone. A seller has the right not to accept an offer under the *Guaranteed Cash Offer* program.

ABOUT KRIS LINDAHL

KRIS LINDAHL is the founder and CEO of Kris Lindahl Real Estate, an innovative, nationally recognized real estate brokerage that typically helps over 4,000 families a year.

Kris earned a bachelor's degree in education, then grabbed an opportunity in the real estate industry and never looked back. After securing his real estate license, he became Minnesota's top real estate agent and led the state's #1 real estate team (RealTrends) before creating the *Guaranteed Cash Offer* program in 2017. Since 2009, thousands of people have trusted him with their real estate transactions.

In May 2018, Kris' success inspired him to form Kris Lindahl Real Estate (KLRE), allowing him to continue to help individuals and families overcome unique challenges in their lives by being their independent, locally owned real estate brokerage.

As part of that commitment, Kris continues to pave the way to convenience-based approaches for all things real estate. KLRE has earned thousands of five-star reviews on Google and other major review sites, and RealTrends consistently ranks it as one of America's top 10 team-based brokerages. Kris owns multiple companies in the real estate industry. His companies make *Guaranteed Cash Offers* to people from diverse backgrounds, and they're constantly buying houses as part of the *Guaranteed Cash Offer* program.[2]

Kris is a best-selling author, sought-after speaker and mentor, and winner of *The Business Journals'* 40 Under 40. He also founded the Kris Lindahl Foundation, which encourages people to Be Generous and donate their Time, Talents and Treasures to help their communities.

Outside of work, Kris enjoys fishing all over the world and spending time with his daughter, Victoria.

---

[2] To keep things simple, this book may sometimes refer to one or more of Kris' companies as "we" or "our."

I KNOW WHERE YOU'RE COMING FROM

IF YOU'RE READING this book, you're probably dealing with a challenging situation that's causing fear, anxiety, exhaustion or a general feeling of being overwhelmed. Maybe you're facing financial hardship. Maybe you're going through a divorce. Maybe you have an aging relative who's no longer safe living in their house. Maybe you've lost a spouse, the house is too much to take care of and you just need to move on to the next chapter of your life.

As an experienced real estate agent and broker, I've sat down with people of all ages, backgrounds and situations to help them. As a human being, I've also experienced my personal share of challenges, including poverty, housing insecurity, divorce, the early death of my father and inheritance issues leading to family stress.

Along the way, I've been fortunate to meet coaches, teachers, friends and mentors who took the time to listen, understand my challenges and lend a helping hand. That's what I want to do for you with this book. I want to save future home-sellers like you from making the mistakes I've seen so many homeowners make over my career.

I shifted my focus from teaching to real estate when I realized the importance of "home," but I'm still an educator at heart. I want to teach you that a house should be an asset, not a liability. It should help you, not cause you stress. It should give you energy, not drain it. And it should add to your life and your freedom, not take away from it.

I see myself in many of the situations I'm about to describe, and I hope I've managed to capture where you're at as well. If you're dealing with life's many challenges, and you need a quick way out, a smart way forward or a little bit of both, then this book of never-before-shared information is for you.

Some people who've already sold their house will read this book and wish they could go back in time and accept a *Guaranteed Cash Offer* instead. Don't let this happen to you! By the time you turn the last page, you'll better understand your options. You'll better understand the benefits of a *Guaranteed Cash Offer*, how to avoid paying a dime in commissions and how to avoid the regret that some people experience when they sell a different way. In short, you'll learn how to feel great about how you sell your house.

GIVE YOURSELF A PAT ON THE BACK

BEFORE WE START, congratulations! Just by opening this book, you've already done a difficult thing and are miles ahead of everyone else.

You're taking an important step *forward*, and that's where I've been taking real estate for years. I've never understood why selling a house is so slow and inconvenient compared to other transactions, and why it has changed so little in a century.

Imagine going back to a world where you had to wait for the morning paper to find out who won last night's game. A world with pay phones, but no smart phones. Taxis, but no rideshare cars. Libraries, but no internet.

Crazy, right?

Today, we can buy virtually anything we want with a click. We're loyal to any brand that saves us time, lowers our risk, and gives us more certainty and less hassle. So why do we still live in the 1950s when it comes to selling houses?

Why do we assume that it'll take weeks or months for us to close on a property sale instead of being able to do it fast?

Why do we have to move out of a house on the same day we close, instead of getting cash today and moving later?

Why do we risk injury and spend thousands of dollars and hundreds of hours to clean, declutter, remodel and repair our houses — only to have buyers tell us that we did everything wrong?

Why do we put signs in our yard broadcasting our property sale to neighbors, forcing us to admit the next time we see them at the grocery store that we lost our job or are going through a divorce?

Why do we let family dinners turn into fire drills that force us to pack up our kids and pets whenever someone wants to see our house?

And why do we let a parent's death or move to senior housing lead to family strife when it comes to dealing with their house?

By reading this book, you're saying, "I know there's a better way, one that fits me and my situation." I'm on that mission too.

Give yourself a pat on the back for not accepting the status quo and being open to doing things differently. I'm confident that it will pay off for you in more ways than one.

INTRODUCTION

I MOVED SEVEN times before I was 12 years old. The reasons are complicated and worthy of their own book (I'm writing that one as well). But the point is, I know what it's like to face the consequences of divorce, job loss, financial hardship, impending foreclosure, a death in the family, you name it.

Many of you reading this book find yourself (or someone close to you) in similar situations. For whatever reason, you have to move out of your house soon. It would be nice to have $50,000 sitting in the bank to cover the work you need to do to sell it, but that's not the case.

Instead, the clock is ticking and you need another option. You've seen our billboards, TV and radio commercials, banner ads, bus wraps and other marketing materials promoting the *Guaranteed Cash Offer* program. You've known about Kris Lindahl Real Estate for years. And you can definitely put a face to the name (as well as two long arms).

But lately, you've also seen new places that sound like they offer something similar, and you're curious.

I'm writing this book for a lot of people in diverse situations, but I'm writing it especially for *you*. Based on my extensive experience as a real estate agent and broker, I have a good idea of what you do and don't want.

⇒ You want a fair and competitive offer on your house.

⇒ You want a process that's simple and fast.

⇒ You want to work with friendly, trustworthy people who will listen carefully to your situation and offer a solution that helps you move on to the next phase of your life.

⇒ You don't want to be insulted.

⇒ You don't want to feel judged.

⇒ You don't want to feel like someone is trying to take advantage of you.

⇒ You don't want to wait or procrastinate.

⇒ You don't want to feel paralyzed or helpless.

In short, you want *relief*.

I've seen too many people fall into the trap of letting acquisition companies they don't know much about enter their lives. Too often, they've been burned, ignored, lowballed, insulted or abandoned.

More and more so-called "real estate investors" emerge every day. They tout their interest in buying homes in your area. They might come in hot with big advertising budgets. They could be companies or individuals saying things like "here's how to buy a house with no cash." And then many of them seem to disappear as quickly as they emerged.

When you're selling a house, you want to work with someone you can trust to follow through on what they promise. Chances are, you know my name and face, and that I've been in real estate for a long time. You've probably seen and heard us online, on TV, on the radio and on the highway for years. KLRE has earned thousands of five-star reviews on Google and other major review sites, and RealTrends consistently ranks us as one of the top 10 team-based brokerages in the U.S.

I created the original *Guaranteed Cash Offer* program in 2017 because I realized that for a growing number of homeowners, the system for selling a house no longer fit their needs. If you expose yourself to the old-fashioned "open market" way of selling, you might find yourself spending a crazy amount of time and money on repairs, renovations, showings and open houses. You might also lose days of sleep, spend every day feeling anxious and uncertain, and wind up losing 10% of the sale to commissions and closing costs.

> **Open-Market Selling**
>
> Selling your house the old, slow way. Constantly negotiating. Hiring an agent. Arranging showings and open houses. And then paying commissions and closing costs.

Selling a house doesn't have to be such a stressful experience. We live in The Golden Age of Convenience. We can access information instantly. We can tap a growing number of AI resources. We can buy anything, from a loaf of bread to a car, with a click.

Accepting a *Guaranteed Cash Offer* feels that easy. It's convenient. It's commission-free. You get your offer fast. You choose your closing date and moving dates (they don't have to be the same!). You can even outsource your packing and moving. If you don't like risk or uncertainty, it can be a refreshing option.

The world has changed; the real estate industry just hasn't realized it yet. It's time to talk about the pitfalls and relentless stress of exposing yourself and your house to the open market.

More importantly, it's time to share the benefits of the *Guaranteed Cash Offer* program that has taken the country by storm and inspired so many pale imitations from coast to coast.

Maybe it's because of how I grew up, but I've always been passionate about helping people sell their properties with dignity, speed and convenience. It's one of the reasons why Kris Lindahl Real Estate has earned thousands of five-star reviews on Google and other major review sites and has become such a household name in our markets.

You already know our billboards, banner ads, sponsorships and yard signs. With this book, I want you to know your *choices* so you can make a decision that fits your situation and your personality.

After reading this book, you might be tempted to ignore what you've learned and go back to your comfort zone. That's one of the reasons why a *Guaranteed Cash Offer* isn't for everyone. You have to be open-minded about change, and some people are more set in their ways.

Once you share what you've learned here, will your friends and family members in real estate be skeptical? Of course! "Why would you give your house away?" they might say, because they're threatened by any fresh idea that might erode their commissions.

My mission here is simple. I grew up in a financially challenged household where we were forced to move constantly. I learned to value "home" at an early age. I also benefited from teachers, coaches and other mentors who believed in me and gave me a helping hand.

Now I want to mentor *you*. I'm going to compare apples to apples so you can decide the path that's right for you. And I'm going to share my industry knowledge with you so you never have to think, "I wish I would have sold my house differently."

Lastly, whether you live in an urban, suburban or rural neighborhood, please know that accepting a *Guaranteed Cash Offer* may be a viable option for you. It's an option for *anyone* who wants to avoid exposing their house to a potentially slow-moving and constantly changing open market.

Ready to get started? Let's do it! I *guarantee* that you'll find insights in these pages that will surprise and inspire you.

GLOSSARY OF TERMS

Appraisal Nightmare: What you enter when your potential buyer's mortgage lender appraises your property lower than the buyer's offer. (Only happens on the open market, not when you accept a *Guaranteed Cash Offer*.)

Cash Closing Date: The date you pick to close on your *Guaranteed Cash Offer*. If you want to stay in the house longer, you don't have to move on the same day as your Cash Closing date.

Contingency Limbo: When you buy your next house on contingency, then your purchase falls apart because your buyer backed out.

Days on Market Disease: When your property sits on the open market and potential buyers start to think, "What's wrong with that house?"

Deadbeat Rental Property: When a rental property you own is losing money every month because your current tenants have stopped paying, you can't afford to repair damages or make updates, or the rental laws in your area have changed.

Holding Costs: The cost of keeping your house on the open market as you try to sell it, including the mortgage, property taxes, escrow, insurance, utilities, lines of credit, property management and, depending on your climate, seasonal maintenance.

Inflated Valuation Syndrome: When you trust an inflated valuation of your house that you see online or on your property tax statement.

"Just Tell Me the Number" Syndrome: The tendency of many homeowners who request a *Guaranteed Cash Offer* to say "just tell me the number." This is a sure sign that the person doesn't understand the full value of a *Guaranteed Cash Offer*.

Open-market Selling: Selling your house the slow and old-fashioned way most people are used to, involving agents, showings, open houses, and paying commissions and closing costs.

WHAT IS A *GUARANTEED CASH OFFER?*

A *GUARANTEED CASH OFFER* is a process for selling your property that centers on convenience, not commissions. Specifically, it aims to trade red tape, risk, volatility, hassle and exposure for speed, certainty, stability, simplicity and discretion.

A *Guaranteed Cash Offer* is like trading in your old car when you buy a new one: You're not expected to wash it or get it detailed. The buyer takes it "as is."

The process is quick and easy. If you accept your offer, you can close fast, get your cash, then move later when it's more convenient. In some cases, you can even live in the house for free while you look for your next residence!

Why would I want to avoid the "open market" in selling my house?

When I talk about selling your house on the "open market," I mean selling it the traditional way we're all used to. Agents. Signs in the yard. Open houses. Commissions. It's all about having *more* showings to find *more* buyers. This approach has been around so long, most people don't know there's even another option!

There's a reason so many homeowners are accepting *Guaranteed Cash Offers*, and there's a reason so many top agents are reaching out to join our company to help people accept a *Guaranteed Cash Offer* on their house: They know it's the future.

The truth is, the open market also exposes you and your house to potential risk, uncertainty and volatility. Property values, mortgage interest rates, inflation, the cost of living, credit card and student loan debt, the overall economy — these factors can dramatically affect the success you have in selling your house. As we'll talk about later, they can also give you "Days on Market Disease," where the longer your house stays on the market, the more value it loses.

And then even if you *do* sell your house, here come the commissions and closing costs!

If your house is showroom-ready right now and you welcome the risks and expenses of the open market, then a *Guaranteed Cash Offer* probably isn't for you. If, on the other hand, you find yourself in certain life situations, you don't like

paying commissions, or you place a high value on your time and freedom, then a *Guaranteed Cash Offer* can deliver a great value *fast*.

In some cases, your choices are severely limited. Some people can't put their house on the open market because they need cash fast, and doing the work (and paying the money) to get it ready for the open market isn't in the cards. In these cases, accepting your *Guaranteed Cash Offer* can be a highly desirable option.

For others, avoiding the open market frees them from the things they don't like about it: risk, fees, commissions, paperwork, cleaning, decluttering, repairs, photography, staging, open houses and showings.

When did the *Guaranteed Cash Offer* program start?

Our *Guaranteed Cash Offer* program began in 2017. We've been a trusted local presence since 2009, and it's not uncommon for the *Guaranteed Cash Offer* program to generate hundreds of requests in a single month. It's gotten so popular that we now receive offer requests not only for single-family houses but also for multi-family apartments and even undeveloped land.

Some real estate companies claim to offer something similar to the *Guaranteed Cash Offer* program, but don't (see "A *Guaranteed Cash Offer* vs. Other Programs"). We've been around for years. Our companies are constantly buying properties through our program. And we do what we say we're going to do.

11

Do I pay a commission to a real estate agent when I accept a *Guaranteed Cash Offer*?

No.

What's the risk of "testing the market" after I get my *Guaranteed Cash Offer*?

Many homeowners think, "I'll see what my *Guaranteed Cash Offer* is, and if I don't like it, I'll put it on the market." That may sound like going to a brick-and-mortar store to find a TV and then going online to buy it cheaper. But it's not. Here's why.

You probably know a lot of real estate agents, and most are honest people. The truth is that some of them might tell you that your house could sell for more than your *Guaranteed Cash Offer*. What's in it for them? They want to list it. They may want to price it high to get a higher commission for themselves and get the free advertising of putting a sign in your yard.

Here's the problem: If you go on the open market after getting your *Guaranteed Cash Offer*, and your house doesn't sell, then your next *Guaranteed Cash Offer* might face downward pressure. You've given us another data point ("house didn't sell"), and the purchase history leads to a "what's wrong with that house?" perception.

A *Guaranteed Cash Offer* has an expiration date because, like the stock market, the housing market changes day to day, hour to hour. I've seen it happen over and over again: People come back to us only to find that their *Guaranteed Cash Offer* is lower than it was before. (For more on this, see the "Phases of People Who Wait Too Long" chart a few pages ahead.)

What if a *Guaranteed Cash Offer* isn't for me?

It's true: a *Guaranteed Cash Offer* isn't for everyone, especially if your house is already perfect and ready to list. If you have the time, money and motivation to invest in your house, don't need to close fast, aren't in the thick of big life changes and don't mind if your property takes months to sell, then maybe betting on the open market is the way to go.

My hope is that when you're done reading this book, you'll feel confident that you have a choice in how you sell your property, as well as a clearer picture of how much *you* can control the experience.

5 TAKEAWAYS ON ACCEPTING A *GUARANTEED CASH OFFER*

---

1. **The value of your house isn't what you *feel* it's worth or want it to be worth. It's based on analytics and metrics.**

The agents at my companies and I have sat at thousands of kitchen tables with homeowners, and I can tell you this without a doubt: The most critical step toward having success with a *Guaranteed Cash Offer* is getting on the same page on day one about what your property is worth, which repairs and updates need to be made, and how much that work is realistically going to cost. If we don't start with a fact-based value, you might initially feel insulted by the *Guaranteed Cash Offer* number you receive. That's because the number you thought your house was worth was based on emotion, not facts.

My companies have an in-house underwriting department that looks at properties all day, every day, so we're experts in this space. And because we buy and renovate so many properties, we also know exactly what repairs and renovations cost in the real world.

2. **In some situations, accepting your *Guaranteed Cash Offer* may be your only option.**

Do you have $30,000–$50,000 stashed away for when your roof starts to leak or your water heater rusts out? If you don't, or if you need cash quickly for other reasons, then saying yes to your *Guaranteed Cash Offer* can be an attractive option. You get a fair and competitive offer. You don't have to do a thing to your house. You can close quickly and get your cash without having to move out right away. And if you want, you can leave everything behind.

3. **A *Guaranteed Cash Offer* does apply to you and your property.**

If you're highly motivated, need to move quickly or don't have the resources to prepare your house for the open market, then accepting a *Guaranteed Cash Offer* may be for you (see #1). But it's also a great choice for many people who don't necessarily think of it right away.

For decades, many people have assumed that they need to put their house on the open market and pay commissions and closing costs. A *Guaranteed Cash Offer* creates an alternative that many people find attractive. You get a fair and competitive offer, and it's designed for virtually any property that isn't in ready-to-sell condition.

Scan the QR code to apply for your *Guaranteed Cash Offer* fast.

4. Putting your house on the open market might involve far more time, money and stress than you think.

When's the last time you sold a house? Five years ago? Ten? Twenty? Never?

You might not realize how *slow* the old-fashioned process of putting a house on the market feels now. You hire an agent you already know (a friend or family member). Make repairs. Clean and stage. Vacate your house whenever there's a showing or open house. Wait for an offer. Negotiate. Close and pay commissions.

> **Open-Market Selling**
>
> Selling your house the old, slow way. Constantly negotiating. Hiring an agent. Arranging showings and open houses. And then paying commissions and closing costs.

When you sign a listing contract, you also sign up for 50 different jobs and surrender a huge chunk of your freedom. Unless you're a contractor or interior designer, you're probably unprepared for what you're about to experience. I can't count the number of people who've said to me, "If I knew then what I know now, I would have gone with a *Guaranteed Cash Offer*."

5. **The more you don't like risk, the better a _Guaranteed Cash Offer_ looks.**

I've sold billions of dollars in real estate as an agent and broker, and I've seen almost everything that can go wrong along the way. Putting your house on the open market carries potential risks that you might want to avoid. It's a complex process with dozens of moving parts. Each introduces another layer of uncertainty, another chance for emotions to take over and more volatility that could cost you money.

Some people like the feeling of cutting through the red tape and don't want anything to do with the traditional way of selling a house. That's why my companies are constantly buying properties through the _Guaranteed Cash Offer_ program. It's also why Kris Lindahl Real Estate has earned thousands of five-star reviews. Our sellers love the fact that it's fast, they know exactly what they're getting, and they're in control.

DON'T MAKE THIS MISTAKE!

I'VE SEEN IT OVER AND OVER AGAIN. Someone requests a *Guaranteed Cash Offer*, but by the time they're ready to accept it, the offer is lower than it would have been if they'd accepted it right away. These homeowners generally fall into one of the following categories:

- The **Over-Analyzer** never has enough information.

- The **Skeptic** doesn't trust anything or anyone.

- The **Foot-Dragger** can't make big decisions.

- The **Wheeler-Dealer** always wants a better deal.

- The **Comfort-Zoner** goes back to what they know.

- The **Decision-by-Committee** person involves too many people and never comes to a consensus.

19

Phases of People Who Wait Too Long to Accept Their *Guaranteed Cash Offer*

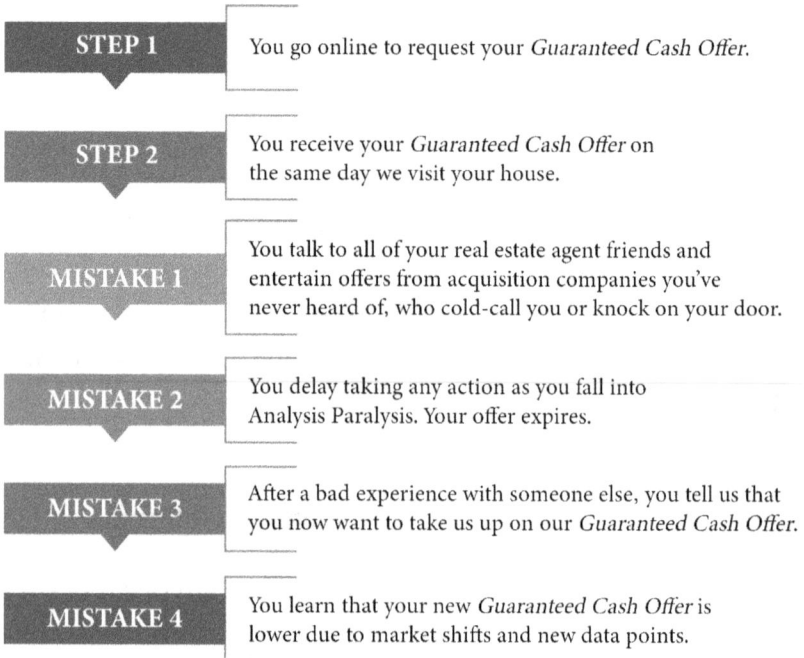

STEP 1 — You go online to request your *Guaranteed Cash Offer*.

STEP 2 — You receive your *Guaranteed Cash Offer* on the same day we visit your house.

MISTAKE 1 — You talk to all of your real estate agent friends and entertain offers from acquisition companies you've never heard of, who cold-call you or knock on your door.

MISTAKE 2 — You delay taking any action as you fall into Analysis Paralysis. Your offer expires.

MISTAKE 3 — After a bad experience with someone else, you tell us that you now want to take us up on our *Guaranteed Cash Offer*.

MISTAKE 4 — You learn that your new *Guaranteed Cash Offer* is lower due to market shifts and new data points.

THE RESULT — **You Lose Money**

BEWARE SHADY IMITATORS!

IF YOU'RE CONSIDERING an alternative way to sell your house, you might feel confused about who you can trust.

Let me help you out.

My companies are constantly buying houses through Kris Lindahl Real Estate's *Guaranteed Cash Offer* program. You've probably seen our billboards, banner ads, TV ads, mail, yard signs and other marketing for years. You might know friends or neighbors who've sold their houses through a *Guaranteed Cash Offer*.

Other organizations may lack that experience and commitment. Some sound like us on the surface, but they're not. Here are three types of places to beware of:

» **The Bait & Switcher.** These companies will make a high cash offer on your property, then later try to force you down to a far lower number. It's a bait-and-switch technique that wastes your time and leaves you in limbo.

» **The Ponzi Schemer.** These places will make a cash offer on your house without actually having the money or resources to close. If you accept the offer, they'll immediately try to sell your property to someone else. If they don't find another buyer before your closing, then they'll back out of the deal, leaving you in a terrible spot.

» **The "If They Can't Sell Your House, They'll Buy It" Company.** These places promise to personally buy your house if they can't sell it in 30 or 60 days. The problem? They may set the listing price too low. They'll expect you to pay for things like staging and repairs. And they may put you through price reductions until your house is massively undervalued.

Kris Lindahl Real Estate is the opposite of these companies. People know our name and have seen our billboards and other ads for years. They've given us thousands of five-star reviews on Google and other major review sites. We're consistently ranked by RealTrends as one of the nation's top team brokerages. And we've received thousands of *Guaranteed Cash Offer* requests.

I created the *Guaranteed Cash Offer*, and I believe that the integrity of our program is unmatched in the industry.

ARE YOU OVERVALUING YOUR PROPERTY?

―――――――――

WE WALK THE *Guaranteed Cash Offer* road to success together from day one, but homeowners often take one wrong turn that sends them down the path of failure: They imagine a value for their house based on what they *want* it to be worth rather than what the market says it's worth.

This is completely understandable. I got into real estate because it's an emotional space. The concept of "home" meant so much to me growing up, and we all tend to overvalue our own spaces.

But when it comes to knowing what your property is worth in the real world, you have to be *fact-based*, not emotion-based.

I've worked with thousands of homeowners who've told me that their home is worth an unrealistic amount. Our conversations go like this:

"Okay, so how did you calculate that value?"
—*"It's what we need to make our next move."*

"Have you looked at comparable houses in your area that have sold in the last 90 days?"
—*"The one on the corner sold for about what we're looking for."*

"Does it have the same square footage, layout, and number of bedrooms and bathrooms as yours?"
—*"No, it's bigger."*

"Is it the same age and in the same condition as yours?"
—*"No, it's newer and in better shape."*

"Have you figured out everything in your house that needs to be repaired and renovated, and did you realistically estimate how much it will cost to hire out that work, because open-market buyers will insist that it be professionally done?"
—*"Like I said, this is the number we need."*

I can't emphasize this enough: If we're not on the same page from the beginning in the *Guaranteed Cash Offer* process, this gap in perception will only widen. Eventually, it will sabotage your success. I've seen it happen.

"That's fine, I'll just sell my house on the open market," you might say. If you do, you might discover that your house is worth a lot less than you thought.

"I'll do a 'for sale by owner' then." I've seen many homeowners try this, only to find that it keeps them up at night because they don't know what they're doing. Many come back to us after experiencing the time, money and stress involved in selling this way.

We're experts when it comes to assessing house values. We know your property's "as is" value because our in-house underwriting department has access to valuation tools not available to the average homeowner. They're experienced professionals who analyze properties all day, every day.

Because my companies repair and renovate so many properties, we also know what it's going to cost to do that work on your house. Frankly, most homeowners are way off on this part of the process. They think they can skip the work when they sell on the open market, then realize they can't. They try to DIY the work, then realize that open-market buyers want it to be professional. Or they hire the work out, and their contractor finds some costly "surprises."

I can't say it enough: Your home valuation has to be based on what the market will bear, not on the number that you need or want. Many of you will disagree with this advice. You won't believe me when I tell you that your first *Guaranteed Cash Offer* may be the most competitive cash offer you're going to get. And you'll choose to roll the dice by selling your house a different way.

25

That's fine. I realize I won't be able to help everyone who's reading this book. But I want to help as many of you as possible. For that to happen, we need to start by acknowledging that we're on this journey together. Our goal is to get you to the next phase of your life with maximum speed and minimal pain. To accomplish that, we need to follow the proven *Guaranteed Cash Offer* process and work together to get you to success.

The great news is this: Once we see a homeowner do the real math — with an accurate as-is value and repair assessment, combined with realistic open-market expenses — we see them experience a lightbulb moment that gets them really excited. "Wow, a *Guaranteed Cash Offer* is a no-brainer!" they say. And they can't wait to get started.

THE TYPICAL HOUSE SALE TO-DO LIST

WHEN YOU SELL your house on the open market, the following is a partial list of everything you need to do, or consider doing.

- ✓ Choose a real estate agent.

- ✓ Sign a listing contract that's usually in the best interest of the agent and includes their commission.

- ✓ Evaluate your curb appeal.

- ✓ Clean carpets.

- ✓ Clean windows.

- ✓ Clean the fireplace.

- ✓ Clean lightbulbs and light switches.

> **Open-Market Selling**
>
> Selling your house the old, slow way. Constantly negotiating. Hiring an agent. Arranging showings and open houses. And then paying commissions and closing costs.

- ✓ Clean blinds.

- ✓ Clean doors and doorknobs.

- ✓ Clean your AC and heating vents.

- ✓ Clean your kitchen tile grout.

- ✓ Clean the stove.

- ✓ Clean the oven.

- ✓ Clean the microwave.

- ✓ Clear your refrigerator of magnets and photos.

- ✓ Store mops, brooms and vacuums.

- ✓ Remove pet food, dishes and litter boxes.

- ✓ Declutter every inch of your house.

- ✓ Organize your pantry.

- ✓ Store unnecessary dishes.

- ✓ Scrub the kitchen sink.

- ✓ Dust all baseboards.

- ✓ Dust all ceiling fans.

- ✓ Add or prune houseplants.

- ✓ Remove most books from shelves.

- ✓ Reduce wall art.

- ✓ Add lamps to dark spaces.

✓ Get rid of scented candles and plug-in air fresheners.

✓ Deal with another nosy neighbor asking why you're moving.

✓ Remove extra leaves from tables.

✓ Buy new bedspreads.

✓ Make sure beds are always made.

✓ Organize all closets.

✓ Generally "depersonalize" your house.

✓ Repair walls, doors, drywall, windows, etc.

✓ Replace doorknobs, curtains, light fixtures.

✓ Repaint one or more rooms.

✓ Touch up scuff marks on walls.

✓ Fix or replace loose handles.

✓ Replace or remove carpeting.

✓ Pay for professional photos.

✓ Redo landscaping.

✓ Replace the roof.

✓ Clean the garage.

✓ Find storage for removed items.

✓ Get rid of pet smells.

✓ Get rid of pet smells again when it doesn't work.

- ✓ Hide your valuables.

- ✓ Track down your title.

- ✓ Make sure no one else has a title to your house.

- ✓ Make sure there isn't a lien on the house.

- ✓ Have a pre-inspection.

- ✓ Determine if you want to act as general contractor.

- ✓ Manage the painters.

- ✓ Manage the demolition crew.

- ✓ Manage the flooring people.

- ✓ Manage the plumber.

- ✓ Manage the electrician.

- ✓ Choose a remodeling/decorating strategy and hope it's right.

- ✓ Determine your level of staging.

- ✓ Choose and buy new furniture.

- ✓ Leave your house multiple times with little notice.

- ✓ Secure pet care during showings.

- ✓ Stow away laundry soap and supplies.

- ✓ Install higher-wattage bulbs in the laundry.

- ✓ Sweep and mop all floors.

- ✓ Scrub all bathroom surfaces.

- ✓ Buy new towels to display.
- ✓ Remove items from bath/shower.
- ✓ Replace shower curtain.
- ✓ Replace caulking.
- ✓ Hide all garbage cans and cleaning supplies.
- ✓ Organize all cabinets.
- ✓ Replace rotted exterior wood.
- ✓ Paint exterior areas that are fading or flaking.
- ✓ Sweep all porches, patios and decks.
- ✓ Re-stain decks.
- ✓ Buy additional outdoor furniture.
- ✓ Clean, sweep and declutter garage.
- ✓ Prune all exterior greenery.
- ✓ Weed all yards.
- ✓ Lay down fresh mulch.
- ✓ Mow and edge all lawns.
- ✓ Add flowers where needed.
- ✓ Risk injury while decluttering, packing and moving.
- ✓ Spend hours driving to a title company and signing stacks of paperwork.
- ✓ … Collapse.

THE *GUARANTEED CASH OFFER* TO-DO LIST

- ✓ Fill out a short online form.

- ✓ Receive your *Guaranteed Cash Offer* the same day my company visits your house.

- ✓ Approve the offer.

- ✓ Choose a closing date that's convenient for you.

- ✓ Sign a handful (not a stack) of papers that we bring to you.

- ✓ Move out later. We're flexible!

55 SITUATIONS WHERE ACCEPTING A *GUARANTEED CASH OFFER* COULD BE THE SMART THING TO DO

EACH HOMEOWNER'S SITUATION is unique. Most likely, you live in the house you're looking to sell. But at a time when so many people are moving into retirement homes or senior-/ assisted-living facilities, you might also be looking at options to sell a parent's property that you don't currently live in.

After working with thousands of people facing nearly every challenge imaginable, I've identified at least 55 situations where accepting a *Guaranteed Cash Offer* could be the smartest decision for selling your property.

How many of them apply to you? Let's find out.

I. PERSONAL CHALLENGES

THESE SITUATIONS INVOLVE issues that happen to most of us at some point in our lives. Accepting a *Guaranteed Cash Offer* can simplify things to help you get through difficult times more easily.

1. You're going through a divorce.

If you're in the process of ending a marriage or another close relationship, I'm sorry. It's a challenging time, especially when the circumstances surrounding the decision include substance abuse, violence or other traumatic family issues. Even if it's simply a matter of realizing that you and your partner aren't right for each other, the process is emotionally draining. I've been there.

> **Open-Market Selling**
>
> Selling your house the old, slow way. Constantly negotiating. Hiring an agent. Arranging showings and open houses. And then paying commissions and closing costs.

Whatever the circumstances around your divorce, accepting a *Guaranteed Cash Offer* instead of exposing your house (and your relationship) to the open market is a popular and attractive option. It doesn't matter if it's *you* going through the divorce or your parents. Whether the situation is amicable or contentious. Whether one person has already moved out of the house or both parties still live there. Privacy is key.

When you expose your house to the open market, the neighbors know what's going on. They see the "for sale" sign in the yard. They see the house listed online. They see contractors and buyers entering and exiting. Soon the whispers and rumors start. Maybe some nosy neighbors go to your open house because they're curious about "how those people lived."

This is hard enough for any couple getting divorced; it can be even harder for their kids. They already have to deal with their parents splitting up. The last thing they want is to get sideways glances from friends and neighbors or be asked invasive questions.

From the divorcing (or separating) couple's perspective, putting their house on the open market prolongs the amount of time they have to keep communicating — and paying their attorneys. Some divorces are more contentious than others. But across the spectrum, most couples would rather not have to deal with house issues and legal bills any longer than they have to.

Also, keep in mind that both people getting divorced have a legal interest in any jointly owned property. They're both usually named in the mortgage and the title. In other words, if your soon-to-be ex-spouse tries to keep your house while you move somewhere else, you're still liable if they fail to pay the mortgage or if something goes wrong with the house. That will also make it harder for you to qualify for a new loan.

When you accept your *Guaranteed Cash Offer*, you create a fresh start for all parties involved in a divorce. It gets you on the same page by guaranteeing that the house will be sold. It reduces the amount of time you have to talk to each other. And because it's not a long, drawn-out open-market strategy, it typically lowers the cost of attorney bills.

But the most underrated benefit of a *Guaranteed Cash Offer* is *privacy*. There's no sign in the yard. No agents getting involved in your family's personal life. No contractors. No buyers. The neighbors don't know the house has changed ownership until the moving trucks show up.

Bottom Line

If you or your parents are going through a divorce, you want to avoid complicated legal and financial issues. You also don't want a long, drawn-out process that makes the whole neighborhood gossip about your family's personal life. Better to get everyone on the same page with a *Guaranteed Cash Offer*, make the house go away before anyone knows it's for sale and feel free to move on to the next chapter of your life.

2. You've had a death in the family.

Perhaps no situation creates more conflict, confusion and hurt feelings than a death in the family, especially the death of a partner. I've experienced it myself. My dad died suddenly when I was in high school. Dealing with the shock and grief was hard enough. But the conflicts over possessions and property that came later were the last thing anyone in our family needed.

Unfortunately, this happens often, especially when the deceased didn't have a will. The same people who stood shoulder to shoulder at the funeral start fighting over who gets control of what, especially the house. Cousins and other relatives you've never met or haven't seen in years come out of the woodwork. Then look out: Here come the lawyers!

Even if your family is getting along, you might be avoiding selling the house because it feels easier in the short run. You might think you need to wait for the probate process. Or you might be in the process of cleaning out the house, which produces its own pain and difficulties.

I'm not here to claim that accepting a *Guaranteed Cash Offer* has the magic ability to erase grief or make familial conflicts and avoidance go away. But in my experience as an agent and broker, it *can* provide helpful solutions and make things a heckuva lot easier.

For partners, it alleviates the loneliness you might feel now that your other half is no longer there. It helps you transition to the next chapter of your life. And it gives you more energy and excitement around taking that next step.

In general, accepting your *Guaranteed Cash Offer* can eliminate stress and infighting over which real estate agent you're going to hire, how you should price the house, which updates and repairs should be made (and how much money should be put toward them), what to do with your family member's possessions, and who's going to lead the entire massive project.

Finally, if you're in the middle of cleaning out your relative's house as you're reading this, press pause. You might not have to go through that physical and emotional pain, because we may be able to take care of it for you. So many people call us after they've already cleaned everything out of their relative's house. I always wish they had called sooner, because our program could have saved them all that stress around cleaning and packing.

When you accept your *Guaranteed Cash Offer,* you simply sign the paperwork, get the money from the sale and divide it any way you'd like. If everyone's busy and doesn't have time to clean everything out, no worries! If you want, you can leave everything behind, and we'll handle it.

Because of my personal experience with this issue, I also know the importance of families assigning a central point of communication. The more family members involved on your end, the more critical it is to have only *one* person representing them with the real estate company. Again, simplicity rules the day.

Bottom Line

The death of a partner or family member should be about remembering and celebrating the person who has passed, not dealing with the pain of packing their belongings and getting into disputes over money and property. Especially if you come from a big family, accepting your *Guaranteed Cash Offer* can save you invaluable time and stress — not to mention attorney fees.

3.   Your house is in disrepair.

Before you say "this one doesn't apply to me," keep reading. "Disrepair" doesn't necessarily mean your house is falling down. The real estate industry's definition of disrepair can simply mean that your property is outdated by the standards of current consumer tastes.

Some homeowners know their house is in disrepair and know that they don't have the time or money to fix it. They just need to sell the property fast without doing anything to it.

Others think "in disrepair" means "unlivable." The house is livable to them, so they assume it's also livable to everybody else and not in disrepair. But when they put it on the open market and receive feedback from potential buyers, they learn that it has tons of problems they don't have the time or money to fix.

Still others have relocated for work, or will be shortly, and find managing their property's condition from afar next to impossible. Getting their house out of a "disrepair" state is going to be a huge challenge.

The truth is, most homeowners simply don't know that their house is in a state of disrepair. In my career as an agent and broker, I've talked to countless homeowners who claimed to have kept their properties clean and well maintained, but have missed the importance of updating. Our conversations go something like this:

*"So which rooms have you remodeled
over the last five years?"*
—*"None."*

"Have you redone the kitchen?"
—*"No."*

"How about the bathrooms?"
—*"No."*

They're surprised when I tell them that, according to current industry standards and consumer expectations, their house is "in disrepair." When they start doing the math on the time and money needed to get the house up to "open market" standards, they feel overwhelmed and don't know where to start.

If this describes your situation, then accepting your *Guaranteed Cash Offer* can give you a viable alternative to spending months (and tons of money) removing the "disrepair" label from your house.

ADDITIONAL RESOURCE!

Use our offer calculator to get your initial offer now without talking to a salesperson. Just scan the QR code below.

Instead, you can leave your house "as is" and get a cash offer. Will that offer be as high as one you might receive after getting your property in an ideal "showroom" state? Not likely. But when you add up the costs of repairs and updates, place a value on the time and stress involved in getting them done, and include the commissions and

© 2024 Lindahl Realty LLC

fees you'll have to fork over in a traditional selling model, accepting your *Guaranteed Cash Offer* looks more and more attractive.

Bottom Line

Some people own property that's in such disrepair they simply need to sell it fast. Others radically overestimate the condition of their house and are surprised when the market considers it to be in "disrepair." When you accept your *Guaranteed Cash Offer*, you give yourself a smart way to sell without having to invest one second or dollar removing the "disrepair" label.

4. You need to relocate.

Remote work and hybrid work options are popular, but people still need to relocate for their jobs. When that happens, the stress goes up exponentially.

Relocation saddles you with a hard deadline. You need to find a new house in a new place. Maybe your employer is helping you; maybe they're not. Either way, you'll soon have another mortgage or rent to pay, and you don't want to pay for two at the same time.

You also have limited time to get your current house ready for the open market. With all the chaos of moving and changing jobs, the last thing you want to think about is cleaning, repairing, decluttering and staging.

On top of all that, you don't want the added inconvenience of keeping your property spotless 24/7 and vacating for showings at a moment's notice. If you also have young kids and pets, forget about it.

Accepting your *Guaranteed Cash Offer* may give you an attractive option for work relocations. It removes the uncertainty and puts you in control. You choose when to sell. You choose when to close. You choose when to move. You don't have to lift a finger to get your house ready. All you have to do is focus on the future and build your new life in your new location.

Bottom Line

If you need to relocate for work or other reasons, accepting your *Guaranteed Cash Offer* dramatically simplifies and streamlines the process of selling your house. Because it delivers a cash offer the same day we meet and lets you choose your closing date (we call it your Cash Closing date), as well as your moving date, a *Guaranteed Cash Offer* makes your relocation faster and more convenient.

5. There's tension in the family over a parent's property.

As people age, their properties can become huge sources of conflict within families. If you're not already experiencing some of this yourself, here's what I mean.

Say something happens to one or both of the parents in a family. The kids have to deal with the house, and they all have different ideas about what to do. One thinks you should sell it, which means getting rid of tons of stuff. Another wants to keep it, fix up the kitchen and rent it out. Still another wants to live in it. No one can agree. Everyone is stuck.

Or say one parent is still alive and living in the house. One sibling does most of the caregiving and knows that the parent should move into senior housing. Another sibling, who lives out of town, hears a different story from the parent that leads to conversations with their sibling like this:

> *"I talked to Mom last night, and she was crying. Why are you forcing her to move?"*
>
> —*"You don't see her every day. It's not safe for her to be living in that house."*

> *"She sounded fine when I talked to her. She's just upset that you keep telling her what to do."*
>
> —*"Then why don't you move here and take care of her yourself?" Click.*

Sound familiar?

For kids and grandkids, watching a family member stay too long in their house can cause a lot of pain. Just as some families need to have hard conversations about taking away a relative's driver's license so they don't harm themselves or others on the road, it can be even harder to talk about "taking the house away" and moving them into senior or assisted living.

Most homeowners do not consciously want to leave a mess for their children and grandchildren to clean up. But they can also live in denial until a fall or other accident inside the property throws everyone into crisis mode.

From an emotional standpoint, some people refuse to move because they're so attached to their house. It might be the only one they ever bought and the place where they raised their kids.

From a practical standpoint, repairs and decluttering often delay the inevitable. The homeowners won't do it — or physically can't do it — so it falls to the kids and grandkids. They procrastinate because they have fond memories of the house or because they think

> **ADDITIONAL RESOURCE!**
> Parents' and grandparents' properties are such an important issue, I've created an ebook to help everyone navigate the process as smoothly as possible. To access it, scan the QR code below.

it'll be too emotionally draining to go through everything. And how can they coordinate the work, especially if they live all over the country?

Another family dynamic we've seen is this: Many times when we meet with someone about a *Guaranteed Cash Offer*, their child or grandchild is present. Some of them look at the offer as part of their inheritance (rather than as a funding source for assisted living, which is more realistic). And they can actually make a challenging situation worse by saying "we already have an offer for $200K, so you have to match it" or "we're only taking x for the house." In most cases, they haven't done the research or received any offers, and these tactics don't help the process or their relative.

There's no magic solution to family issues around a property, but I've seen the *Guaranteed Cash Offer* process get people to stop crossing their arms and start nodding their heads. It's decisive. It allows people to get into better living situations faster. It unlocks equity and gives families more time to tackle repairs and declutter. It frees everyone to move forward.

Bottom Line

Handling a parent's or grandparent's house is one of the toughest things a family has to deal with. Whether you're trying to convince a relative to move into safer housing or you're struggling to handle the million details related to selling their house, accepting your *Guaranteed Cash Offer* simplifies a difficult process. It allows you to close quickly, move when it's convenient for everyone and avoid family conflicts.

6.   This is the first time you've sold a house.

When's the last time you picked up a paintbrush, let alone installed a thousand pounds of drywall? Have you ever sold a house? And how do you handle rejection, especially over and over again?

If you're eager to do the hard labor, face the rejection, pay the commissions and deal with the risk of selling your house on the open market, then you can stop reading this book. You're not the right person to accept a *Guaranteed Cash Offer*.

But in my career as a real estate agent and broker, I've seen thousands of first-time sellers deal with extreme culture shock. Maybe you're in this situation. Buying your first house was easy. You were in a rental, so all you had to do was end your lease and focus on the fun of finding your first dream home.

When it comes time to sell that first property, you're overwhelmed. You want to focus on the next house to buy, but you can't until you deal with everything involved in selling. Suddenly you're wearing 15 different hats and tackling issues you're not equipped for.

What if you do find your next house, but you're not ready to sell your current one? Now you're cramming to fix it up. The bank isn't willing to lend you the full amount for the new property, so you have to make an offer with a contingency clause, making you less likely to get it.

In addition, the #1 axiom of selling that most first-time sellers don't yet understand is this:

The way we live and the way we sell
are two different things.

Whether you currently live in a single-family house, townhouse or condo, look around you. Seems normal, right? Now take a photo of the room you're sitting in and imagine seeing that photo on a website of properties for sale. Look at it as a buyer, not an owner. Chances are, it looks cluttered. Too many couches and chairs and tables. Too much stuff on the ground. Too many plants. Too many things hanging on the wall.

Take more detailed photos of the room you're in, and you'll start to notice things you've been ignoring for years.

"I forgot how much those ceiling beams dip."

"How did that crack in the plaster get there?"

"That brass doorknob is totally corroded."

"Is that smudge on the wall from when our daughter drew on it with a permanent marker in kindergarten?"

And then there's smell. Most homeowners only notice odors in their house after they return from a vacation, but potential buyers notice them immediately. Most smells are costly to get rid of. (More on that later.)

A property for sale needs to look as impressive as possible. Everybody checks out photos online before going to an open house or scheduling a showing. If your house isn't in showroom condition right now, then you have a lot of work to do. If you can't win the online beauty contest, you might be toast. Same if you can't get the cat litter smell out of the basement.

After meeting with thousands of first-time home-sellers, I can confidently say this: They all want to go look at the next house. They don't want to get theirs ready.

Accepting a *Guaranteed Cash Offer* solves this problem. As a first-time seller, you can concentrate on your *next* house, not your current one. You can sell your house, get your cash, and even stay in your original while you find exactly what you're looking for in the next one. The key: accepting your *Guaranteed Cash Offer* right away to be non-contingent. That way, when the home you want to buy pops up, you can go for it immediately because your house is sold.

No paintbrushes. No drywall. No moving beds and couches so you can refinish flooring and carpeting. No living out of your car while your home sits on the open market and is busy with showings. No turning your house into a perfect showroom overnight. Accepting your *Guaranteed Cash Offer* can make your second home-buying experience as easy as your first one. Maybe even easier.

Bottom Line

As a homeowner, you can sometimes feel like you're trapped in a vicious circle: When you find the perfect *next* house, you want to make sure your current one is sold. But you don't want to sell the current one until you've already found the next one. Accepting a *Guaranteed Cash Offer* frees you to be non-contingent. You'll never hear that you can't get your next home because your current one hasn't sold. Plus, you won't have to worry about feeling rushed. You can stay in the previous house for a bit and move when it's convenient for you.

7. You're upsizing or downsizing.

Whether your plan is to move to a bigger property or a smaller one, putting your house on the open market can present some challenges.

Say you're upsizing because you need more space for your growing family. How are you going to keep your house in showroom condition when you have kids and pets running around? How about getting everyone packed up and out the door quickly? What are you going to do with all the toys lying around? How are you going to get the dogs out of the house? And what if you get a showing alert when it's past your kids' bedtimes?

Now let's say you're downsizing. You want to go from a 3,000-square-foot house to a condo, apartment or co-op that's half the size and has minimal stairs. Where's all your stuff going, and who's making those decisions?

When you expose your house to the open market, you have to get your stuff ready and/or removed immediately. Your stager or agent gives you a list of everything you need to get done. You try to piecemeal it. Then 4, 10, even 14 months later, you realize that for every item you've removed, two more have taken its place. You're spinning your wheels, and you're totally overwhelmed.

Now let's say you have a 4,000-square-foot suburban rambler, and you want to downsize for retirement. You go the *Guaranteed Cash Offer* route. You get your offer fast. You have all the time you need to make your stuff go away, or you can leave it behind for us to deal with. Take what you want, leave what you don't.

Doesn't that sound better?

Bottom Line

Whether you're downsizing or upsizing, exposing your house to the open market creates storage headaches, especially if you have kids or pets. Accepting your *Guaranteed Cash Offer* washes those problems away and streamlines the entire process.

8. You and your partner need help getting on the same page.

Selling a house has a way of bringing out tensions between couples. Oftentimes, one person thinks it's worth more than the other. Or one of you is ready to move into a co-op, senior living or assisted living, and the other one isn't. Maybe you feel sentimental about the house, but your partner has never liked it. Maybe you're willing to sell *only* if you move to the suburbs, and your partner is willing to sell *only* if you stay in the city.

Or maybe the disagreements are smaller: One of you wants a house with a big garage. The other wants a house with a big kitchen. You can't even hammer out those priorities because you're so stressed about selling the current property. Plus, your agent just told you to pack, declutter and complete repairs in the next few weeks.

The additional stress this creates when you're trying to get on the same page with your partner can be a huge problem. Disagreements lead to procrastination and avoidance, which can lead to more disrepair and stress, and result in you staying in your house longer than you should. I've seen it happen over and over again.

Couples in these situations want one part of the process to be simple. That's where a *Guaranteed Cash Offer* comes in.

Accepting a *Guaranteed Cash Offer* doesn't solve every conflict, but it does remove one huge variable. It frees you and your partner to have conversations about the future instead of arguing over the past. Your house sells. You pick your Cash Closing date and your move date. Now you know exactly how long you have to resolve your other conflicts.

Bottom Line

By involving so many decisions and so many players, exposing your house to the open market can make conflicts between couples worse. Accepting your *Guaranteed Cash Offer* helps you focus on the future by simplifying the most important first step: selling your current property fast, with minimal stress and maximum convenience.

A *GUARANTEED CASH OFFER* VS. OTHER PROGRAMS

LET'S BE HONEST: Some people think a *Guaranteed Cash Offer* is only for people who own crappy houses. Not true. It's actually more about the life situation you're in than the condition of your property.

Most acquisition companies are above board. But if you live in a part of the country where shady roofing companies appear out of nowhere and go door to door in your neighborhood after a storm, you might be familiar with "storm chasers" who focus more on making the sale than doing high-quality work. The real estate industry has companies and individuals who also fit this general mold — cold-calling, knocking on doors and throwing out lowball offers that aren't based on real data and market forces.

I've been in many situations where I've said to a homeowner, "Look, I know you want $480K for your house, but the market is selling properties in this neighborhood and condition for more like $250K. I can tell you aren't ready for that, and I don't want to give you a number that'll make you want to punch me in the face. I want to help you, not insult you. So I'm going to leave, and when things change, let me know."

Some acquisition companies don't do this. In fact, sometimes the "buyer" is an individual — someone you know who claims to be a real estate investor but has no idea what they're doing. They might give you a number you find insulting, and in some cases, they won't even have the resources or expertise to follow through on closing.

Outfits like this can come and go. They can even shut down one corporate entity and open up a new one to help shield them from fulfilling their promises.

From time to time, these acquisition companies have also attempted to use our messaging to sell their programs. Don't fall for it! Kris Lindahl has been a trusted local name in real estate since 2009. We have the track record. The rankings. The testimonials. The five-star reviews. If you want to sell quickly and stress-free, then consider the original, exclusive *Guaranteed Cash Offer* program as your next step.

A *Guaranteed Cash Offer* comes from a positive place. We ask, "How can we make selling your house as quick and easy for you as possible?" We pride ourselves on having empathy for all homeowners and recognizing that in addition to speed, few things in life are more valuable than the three Cs of certainty, control and convenience.

If you're facing financial challenges or need to move quickly, accepting a *Guaranteed Cash Offer* might be your most attractive option.

II. AVOIDING HASSLES

THESE SITUATIONS ARE relevant to anyone who values speed and convenience. They're not as serious as a divorce or a death in the family, but they're cases where accepting your *Guaranteed Cash Offer* can save you time and relieve stresses that you might not even know about — especially if this is the first time you've sold a house or you haven't sold one in a long time.

9.   You have pets.

Most people are surprised when I tell them the huge role that pets play in selling houses. But when you put your property on the open market, having pets can lead to some challenging situations:

» You get a notification on your phone that you have to leave in the next 30 minutes for a showing. What are you going to do with your dogs?

» You've spent months getting your house ready to sell, and your dog knows something's up. Right before your big open house, he starts destroying things and relieving himself all over the place.

» You've secured a buyer, then at the last minute they contact your agent and say, "I didn't realize the current owner had cats. The house smells and I'm allergic, so I'm rescinding my offer."

Accepting your *Guaranteed Cash Offer* removes these risks by eliminating showings and open houses. You and your pets aren't stressed over an impending move. And you'll never have an offer rescinded due to allergies or house smells. (More on smells in the next chapter.)

Bottom Line

Pets are a wildcard in selling a house on the open market, and they can create unexpected inconveniences that sabotage a sale. Accepting your *Guaranteed Cash Offer* keeps the pets in your life a source of love and joy, not stress.

10. You don't want to "de-smell" your house.

We just talked about pet smells. Do you smoke? Do you cook exotic meals? Have you had flooding issues? Then your house probably smells for those reasons as well. You've stopped noticing it. But for a potential buyer, smells are the first thing they'll notice when they step inside your house. And it's an instant deal-breaker.

When it comes to odors, pets are just the tip of the iceberg. Buyers are incredibly sensitive to general smells throughout a house and odors unique to certain rooms. In addition to pet smells, we're talking smoke, mold, mildew, gas, garbage, food and cooking odors, and some smells that no one can quite place or describe.

If potential buyers are consistently turned off by a smell in your house, don't be surprised if it turns out to be something you can't fix by simply opening the windows, spraying some air freshener or baking a loaf of bread.

In my career as a real estate agent and broker, I can think of times where banks had financing concerns due to smell issues (usually mold). I've also seen homeowners forced to hire professionals to remove and replace their carpeting, sand the sub floors and get down to the studs to achieve complete odor abatement. The more work they do to remove smells, the more surprises and needed repairs they might find. Thousands of dollars later, they're wondering if they could have avoided all that hassle and expense.

They could have if they'd gone the *Guaranteed Cash Offer* route. Just like other repairs and renovations, accepting your *Guaranteed Cash Offer* transfers responsibility for odor abatement to us. You wash your hands of it. We clean up everything else.

Bottom Line

The longer you've lived in your house, the more you've learned to ignore the way it smells. When you try to sell it, however, odors can become a huge stinking, er, *sticking* point

© 2024 Lindahl Realty LLC

with buyers. When you accept your *Guaranteed Cash Offer*, odor abatement becomes our problem, and you come out smelling like a rose!

11. You don't want to time a sale with a move.

Timing is often the single biggest headache involved in selling a house. Maybe you need the funds from the sale of your current property to finance your next one. Or maybe you're trying to time a sale with availability in a co-op or a senior-living or assisted-living facility, and there's so much demand that it's getting harder and harder to get in.

Traditionally, most of the timing has been out of your control. Maybe you find your next living situation right away, but you can't sell your current house, so you lose your chance to find an ideal next living situation.

Maybe you sell your house, but tight inventories keep you from finding the next residence. Maybe you land a great buyer, only to find out that a job situation or school calendar is forcing them to close sooner than you'd hoped. Or maybe it all works out, but then you have to deal with the hassle of moving in and out on the exact same day.

Finally, you might just procrastinate and not sell at all because it sounds like a pain or the timing never feels right. After all, it's always either a "buyer's market" or a "seller's market," and guess what? You're both a buyer *and* a seller.

A *Guaranteed Cash Offer* is all about timing and flexibility, and *you're in control*. Once you accept your *Guaranteed Cash Offer*, you're free to be non-contingent to buy another house, and free to reserve that spot in a senior-living facility before somebody else does. You pick your Cash Closing date. And, most importantly, you work with us to pick your *moving* date. After receiving your money, you can stay in your house for a period after closing so you don't have to squeeze everything into one chaotic day.

Bottom Line

Timing is difficult when you put your house on the open market, especially if you're also looking for another place to live. You'll rarely, if ever, get the timing exactly right. Accepting your *Guaranteed Cash Offer* puts you in control. You choose when to get your offer, when to close and when to move.

12. You don't want to deal with moving at all.

Moving out of a house is a deeply emotional experience. It's also mentally and physically exhausting. Sometimes you're overwhelmed by the thought of it, or maybe a parent has had a health-related event and needs to move into a safer, healthier place. Whatever the situation, everybody's already coping with a major change in life. Do you really want to think about hauling boxes and moving couches on top of that, especially as you get older?

Now imagine a process for selling your house that places the ultimate premium on speed and convenience. The people who work with you understand what you're going through and try to remove as many stresses and headaches from your life as possible — including moving.

One of the greatest benefits of accepting a *Guaranteed Cash Offer* is that it isn't a one-size-fits-all system. You can choose your level of convenience. Want to avoid cleaning, decluttering, photography and showings? Choose one option. Want to take convenience to the next level and have someone else do your packing and moving for you? There's an option for that too.

We may be able to arrange a maximum-convenience product in which we'll coordinate with professional movers to literally do all the heavy lifting for you. This could save you money, because we can leverage our economies of scale with these companies. More importantly, it'll ease your mind, especially if you need to avoid hard labor or move quickly.

> Want to learn more about having someone else pack up and move your (or your parents') stuff? Scan the QR code below.

Whatever your reasons, accepting your *Guaranteed Cash Offer* gets you moving faster and easier. And remember, with a *Guaranteed Cash Offer*, you can separate your moving date from your Cash Closing date. You don't have to move on the same day you close. And you don't have to move anything!

Bottom Line

Traditionally, selling your house involves hiring movers, doing it yourself, or asking friends and family to help out, which takes time and subjects people to injury. Accepting your *Guaranteed Cash Offer* already allows you to choose your moving date. It can also include an option where we do the packing and moving for you. How great is that?

13. The thought of decluttering makes you break out in hives.

Take a walk through your house. Do you see clutter in every room? Random stuff sitting in the corner? Boxes that need to be moved? Bookshelves that need to be organized?

Do you sense the hours of work it's going to take to fix it all?

Most of us collect a lot of stuff over time, and sometimes putting your house on the open market forces us to become an entirely different person. How do you go from being a hoarder to a declutterer overnight? It doesn't happen.

Most people only declutter when they absolutely have to, like when someone walks in and says, "Um, you have to clean up your junk. Sell things, store them, give them away, recycle them, put them on the curb with a FREE sign, I don't care. But start now!"

When I do consumer workshops, everyone relates to this scenario. It's amazing to see the head nods, laughs and covered faces I get when I bring it up. People know they have too much stuff, or they're in a relationship where one person holds onto things too long and drives their partner crazy.

Decluttering avoidance is also one of the biggest reasons why people procrastinate on selling and eventually find themselves watching someone else snatch up their dream home.

Accepting your *Guaranteed Cash Offer* solves all of that. Many people do it because they're tired of feeling overwhelmed and want a fresh start, free of everything. They also know that if they don't accept their offer right away, they'll keep accumulating more and more stuff, and never be able to break the cycle.

When you accept your *Guaranteed Cash Offer*, you might have to move your stuff eventually, but that doesn't stop you from selling your current house and finding your next one. Because we also separate your Cash Closing date from your move date, you can receive the benefits of a *Guaranteed Cash Offer* before addressing the clutter.

Bottom Line

The overwhelming paralysis you feel at the prospect of decluttering your house is natural, but it shouldn't prevent you from making a smart real estate decision. Accepting your *Guaranteed Cash Offer* removes decluttering as a hurdle in selling your current house and finding your next one. For most people, that's a huge relief.

14. You want to avoid staging and photography.

You've always had to make your house look good before selling it, but today's consumer expectations are off the charts. Your house can't just look decent; it has to look perfect. The internet has raised the bar on making a property look "showroom worthy" with top-notch photography and staging. Many potential buyers won't set foot inside if they aren't blown away online first.

When you see staged vs. unstaged houses online, you instantly know the difference. A properly staged and photographed house has a strategy behind every color and placement. Yet staging is an art form that most people don't understand. They think it's about bringing in tons of furniture and fancy floor lamps. It's actually more about taking things *out* and tapping into buyer psychology online.

Today, properly staging and photographing a house takes extraordinary expertise, time, resources and effort. Imagine going to home improvement and furniture stores to shop for all the staging items you need. Do you have the time? Do you know what to pick up? Are you confident that everything will work for the new buyers coming through?

If you happen to be an interior designer and an architectural photographer all in one, you're in luck! Maybe accepting a *Guaranteed Cash Offer* isn't for you.

But if you haven't sold a house in a long time, or never, then you might be shocked at what's involved. It often means removing most of your items first, so decluttering can be a huge part of the process. Next, your house has to look like a place *buyers* want to live instead of the place where *you've* been living. Do your buyers want carpeting or hardwood floors? Painted or natural brick? Neutral paints or bold? Do you need to rent furniture and accessories? If so, where will you store yours?

Then you need professional photography. I don't care how great your phone is, it's not good enough. More importantly, are you comfortable with your house being photographed at all right now? Will you ever be? For a lot of people, photography is a dealbreaker.

The good news is that accepting your *Guaranteed Cash Offer* totally eliminates the need for staging and photography. We buy "as is." So no need to agonize over hundreds of tiny decisions.

Bottom Line

Staging and photographing your house for today's picky consumer is time-consuming, stressful and potentially expensive. Accepting your *Guaranteed Cash Offer* gives you that valuable time back, eliminating the need to make your house look perfect so it wins the online beauty contest.

15. You don't want to live in a staged house.

What's an even bigger hassle than staging a house? Living in it! Most items in a staged home aren't yours, so they're designed to connect emotionally with potential buyers, not you. They're usually not your style, so your house doesn't feel like "you" anymore.

> **Open-Market Selling**
>
> Selling your house the old, slow way. Constantly negotiating. Hiring an agent. Arranging showings and open houses. And then paying commissions and closing costs.

On the other hand, sometimes homeowners use their own belongings to stage their house on the open market and fail to connect with the most likely new buyers.

Then there's keeping your staged house immaculate all the time. Next to leaving for showings, people who put their houses on the open market cite "incessant cleanliness" as the biggest inconvenience.

Think about how hard it is to keep your house clean in normal times, especially if you have kids, grandkids, nieces, nephews, family visitors and shedding pets. Now imagine keeping it absolutely spotless for days, weeks or months on end.

Imagine keeping the garbage constantly empty. The beds perfectly made. The bathrooms gleaming. The dishes always clean. The kitchen sink always dry. The laundry always done. Imagine doing extensive outdoor maintenance no matter what the season. And don't forget to dust that bowl of fake lemons on the counter!

The way a property needs to look online or for an open house isn't the way anyone actually lives. Accepting your *Guaranteed Cash Offer* relieves you of those obsessive duties. Selling "as is" frees you to be who you are and to live the way you live.

Bottom Line

Traditionally, you have to keep a house you're selling in pristine condition 24/7, to the point where it can feel like you spend more time cleaning than you do living. Accepting your *Guaranteed Cash Offer* frees you from showings and open houses. Put away the sprays, sponges, brooms and mops. Feel free to focus on finding your next property.

16. You want the smoothest possible financing process.

It may sound like I'm stating the obvious, but financing a property purchase is a big deal. The open-market financing process exposes you and your potential buyers to all kinds of potential problems because it creates so much dependency on financing.

A real estate agent in the open market shouldn't be surprised to see 15–25% of accepted offers fall apart before closing due to buyer financing issues. As a seller, that means you could end up moving everything out of your house, only to hear at the last minute that your buyers can't secure financing. Could be a sudden job loss or medical expense. Could be a change in their job status or credit rating. Could be a change in mortgage interest rates, or a bank deciding that, for whatever reason, they no longer want to give the open-market buyer a loan.

When this happens, you're back to the beginning, frantically chasing the market to get your house sold. You have a vacant property that needs significant staging to relist. Prices have likely changed. You have to readjust to all the new listings on the market. Your house has a high "days on market" number. And future buyers are wondering what caused the initial buyers to back out. *Something must be wrong with that house!*

Even if you avoid that situation in the open market, there's still the issue of how much money to get preapproved for. You don't know when your house is going to sell or how much you're going to get for it, so you don't know how much that magical equity check is going to be or when it's going to arrive. Can you get preapproved for $400,000, or do you need to go as high as $700,000? Will anyone give you that kind of money?

Maybe you were counting on $300,000 in equity, but you had to drop the price so many times that you're now only getting $200,000. Or maybe you were way off on your "basis," which happens all the time. You assumed a value for your house that put a certain equity number in your head. Turns out that number was way too high. When you try to line up financing on your next house, the price is suddenly out of reach.

Accepting your *Guaranteed Cash Offer* solves many of these potential financing problems. Once you're approved for an offer, you know your house will sell, and you know exactly how much equity you're going to pocket. Banks love working with people in this situation vs. those who carry dead financial weight.

An added benefit if you plan on buying another house after selling your current one: Accepting your *Guaranteed Cash Offer* puts you in a position of strength with sellers by freeing you to be a "non-contingent buyer." The longer your property lists on the open market with a high "days on market" number, the harder it can be to get another homeowner to accept your offer on their home. When you accept your *Guaranteed Cash Offer*, you don't have to worry about your dream home being gone by the time you finally get an offer on your house.

Bottom Line

Putting your house on the open market can put you in a precarious position with banks. Accepting your *Guaranteed Cash Offer* frees you from the risks of buyers backing out, overvaluing your property, overestimating your equity, not being able to access that equity because you can't find a buyer, and having to buy your next property on a contingency basis.

17. You want to avoid appraisal nightmares.

Here's a scenario I've seen play out more times than I can count: You think you have a slam-dunk deal on your house sale. The buyer's been preapproved. Their offer is solid. You've accepted it. All is well, right?

Wrong.

At this point, your buyer's mortgage lender will conduct an

appraisal on your property to make sure it's worth the offer the buyers made. You can wait weeks to hear back on this appraisal, which means more stress and sleepless nights for you.

Then what if the appraisal comes in low? "I'll just have my own appraisal done," most homeowners think. But that's not how it works. The entire appraisal process is designed to protect the buyer's lender, so they'll only use their own appraisal. Basically, they have all the control, and there's nothing you can do about it.

Why would the appraisal come in low? Simple. The buyer's mortgage lender might notice that other, similar properties for sale in your neighborhood are going for $50,000 less than yours. In that case, they could call the buyer and say, "You know what? We're no longer willing to give you the money you're asking for."

Poof! goes the dream deal; enter the Appraisal Nightmare. Now there's downward price pressure on your house. You have to sell for less, but it still costs too much for the original buyers. So they back out. Other buyers see "price reduction" and wonder what's wrong with your house.

Because a *Guaranteed Cash Offer* is a cash purchase, you don't have to worry about the Appraisal Nightmare. There's only one appraisal — the *Guaranteed Cash Offer* itself — and you can simply say yes or no.

Bottom Line

When you get an open-market offer on your house, it's usually contingent on the buyer getting financing approved, which means your house will have to be appraised by their bank or mortgage lender. If your house appraises lower than your asking price, the open-market buyer will likely either walk away or demand a substantial price reduction. Accepting your *Guaranteed Cash Offer* takes this huge risk off the table.

ARE YOU ASKING
THE WRONG QUESTION?

AS A REAL ESTATE AGENT, the #1 question I used to get from homeowners selling their houses was:

"What's your commission?"

It's human nature to fixate on that one number. But commissions are just one variable in a complicated equation that determines the value of an old-fashioned open-market real estate sale. Other variables include asking price, demand, speed, time and stress.

Creating my *Guaranteed Cash Offer* program took that mindset to the next level: I focused on the overall experience of selling a house, and guess what? I got rid of commissions for *Guaranteed Cash Offer* home-sellers altogether!

In most cases, this removes tens of thousands of dollars in costs for homeowners, which can be the deciding factor in inspiring them to accept their *Guaranteed Cash Offer*.

That's the ultimate beauty of *Guaranteed Cash Offer* sales: They eliminate commissions while also delivering speed, predictability, certainty and convenience.

III. FINANCIAL CHALLENGES

THESE SCENARIOS SPECIFICALLY relate to money issues. Everyone deals with financial stress at some point in their life and struggles with rising costs at every turn. In the situations below, accepting your *Guaranteed Cash Offer* can provide a valuable tool to help solve those challenges or keep them from getting worse.

18. You've had (or anticipate) a sudden change in your job situation.

Do you feel like you're not getting the raises and promotions you deserve? Are you concerned about what your job will look like in the near future? Most people feel both. They want and need higher compensation for their work, but they also worry about their job security. With everything feeling more expensive, they worry that they won't be able to handle their current expenses.

If your employer goes out of business or announces layoffs, will you be able to find another job for the same pay? What if someone across the world can do your job for half the pay? What if AI can do it for almost nothing?

For many people in uncertain job situations, selling their house by putting it on the open market will take too long and cost too much. When you consider the commissions, closing costs, repairs and updates needed, the numbers may not add up. If you need cash quickly, the old-fashioned open market might simply take too much time — generally 2–3 months.[3]

Accepting your *Guaranteed Cash Offer* can offer an attractive alternative. After you complete the application online, you can have cash in hand in a matter of days, not weeks or months. You can stay in the house for a period of time after you close, and we can customize a move-out date that works for you.

It's possible to avoid personal bankruptcy after job loss by accepting your *Guaranteed Cash Offer* and quickly unlocking your home equity. Unfortunately, many people aren't aware of this option until it's too late. Don't let this happen to you.

Bottom Line

It's not uncommon to have an unexpected jolt to your job situation, and many people are feeling increasingly insecure about their ability to maintain current income levels. In addition to potentially requiring more money, selling your house by putting it on the open market can take months to complete. Accepting your *Guaranteed Cash Offer* can shorten the process and can address cash flow challenges *fast*.

---

[3] https://www.krislindahl.com/books/guaranteed-cash-offer-book-notes/

19. You're in debt.

I didn't create the *Guaranteed Cash Offer* only to help people in crisis situations, but it's a great option if you've fallen on hard times and can't get caught up no matter what you do.

We talked about volatile job situations in the previous chapter. Let's look at other common financial stresses:

- Your job is stable, but a stock market crash wipes out a huge chunk of your savings.

- You (or a child or grandchild you've co-signed for or are helping out) have hundreds of thousands of dollars in student loan debt.

- You can no longer afford your car loan or just had to spend your rainy-day fund on a new one.

- Your credit cards are maxed out and your payments are skyrocketing.

- You have a health issue and suddenly face huge medical bills.

- You generally feel like you can no longer keep up with increased expenses in all facets of life.

- You've been behind on your finances for a long time, living paycheck to paycheck and feeling like you're one big event away from losing everything.

- You're concerned about the real estate market crashing and evaporating your equity.

Whatever the circumstances, you need cash.

Do you have at least $50,000 stashed away to make repairs to your house? Probably not. Most people don't. So putting your property on the open market may not be a realistic option for you.

Accepting your *Guaranteed Cash Offer* can get you the cash you need *fast* without throwing you even deeper into debt. Plus, you don't have to move on the day you close. You can get a quick cash infusion, take some time to figure out where you're going to live next and start the process of getting back on track.

Bottom Line

People fall into debt for lots of reasons. Most don't have the time and money to get their home ready for the open market, and most would rather avoid paying commissions and closing costs. Accepting your *Guaranteed Cash Offer* gives you fast access to your equity and puts you in a position to get back in the black. You can even stay in your house for a period of time after you close.

20. You're behind on your mortgage or property tax payments.

I've singled out these two financial challenges because they're the most common forms of debt that homeowners deal with, especially as property values rise. Things are getting tight. If inflation doesn't ease up soon, you might have to choose between spending your limited resources on food, medicine, your mortgage or your taxes.

If you put your house on the open market, this stress only rises in the short term. You don't have money for repairs, updates and landscaping to make your house more attractive to buyers. Do you want to go into more debt by borrowing money to fix up the house when you're not even sure exactly which fixes need to be made?

> **Open-Market Selling**
>
> Selling your house the old, slow way. Constantly negotiating. Hiring an agent. Arranging showings and open houses. And then paying commissions and closing costs.

In addition, your property taxes only seem to be going up with higher valuations every year. You have no idea how long it's going to take to sell your property. And each month you can't sell it means another missed mortgage or tax payment.

Accepting your *Guaranteed Cash Offer* may get you out of this vicious cycle. You can address your immediate problems by selling your house "as is" without investing a penny. You can sell immediately instead of waiting for months. You can get cash now and move later. And you can start to make up the deficit in your mortgage or tax payments.

In the longer term, accepting your *Guaranteed Cash Offer* can get you into a more sustainable housing situation, prevent further damage to your credit rating and protect your long-term financial health.

Bottom Line

If you're behind on your mortgage or property tax payments, exposing your house to the open market will likely push you even closer toward foreclosure. Accepting your *Guaranteed Cash Offer* may remove that risk, free you to sell fast, help you emerge from debt and put you on a path to greater financial stability.

21. You're facing (or in) foreclosure.

Are you so far behind on your mortgage payments that the bank is threatening to foreclose on you?

Did you modify your mortgage to get caught up on payments but are now behind and in foreclosure?

Maybe you're dealing with a property that's in danger of foreclosure due to the death of a relative.

Maybe you refinanced to take cash out of your equity but can't keep up with the payment after the refinance.

Or maybe your mortgage rate has become unaffordable because you previously worked something out with your mortgage company, or a late payment caused them to change their original terms.

I know a lot about foreclosure situations — not because I've faced them myself, but because I started my real estate agent career when foreclosures were rampant during the Great Recession. Based on my experience, the most important thing I can tell you is this:

If you're facing foreclosure, you might have options you're

not even aware of. First, let's talk about avoiding foreclosure, as well as "short sales."[4]

Maybe you bought a house in the last few years, put down only 3%, haven't seen the property value rise and suddenly need to sell because of a job loss or relocation. If you go on the open market, your selling fees may come in at around 10%. Where's the other 7% going to come from? You should consider a *Guaranteed Cash Offer*.

Or maybe you simply overspent on your house. You didn't put much down when you bought it. When the value went up, you took out a home equity line of credit on top of your mortgage. Now you've spent that money, and exposing your house to the open market — with its fees and commissions — will put you in the red. You should get a *Guaranteed Cash Offer*.

By letting you keep the money that might otherwise fall down the sinkhole of commissions and closing costs, accepting your *Guaranteed Cash Offer* may help you avoid foreclosure in these situations. So, depending on your exact situation (e.g., we can't make an offer on a house that's "upside down" with a mortgage bigger than it's worth), accepting your *Guaranteed Cash Offer* is an option worth considering.

If you're dealing with a house that's in danger of foreclosure after the death of a relative — and the house has equity — you might assume that you'll have to pay a lot of money to take legal

---

[4] Taking an offer on your house at a lower asking price than what you owe on your mortgage. Short sales require a heavy time commitment. You have to gather tons of documents, then potentially wait months to find out if the bank will consider a short sale vs. foreclosing on your loan.

ownership of it so you can sell it. Not necessarily. In that situation, a *Guaranteed Cash Offer* might open up other options for you, so talk to us right away to learn more.

If you're already in foreclosure, you can still accept a *Guaranteed Cash Offer* while you're in the redemption period. We're experts in helping with this, and we're seeing homeowners in foreclosure accept a *Guaranteed Cash Offer*, close on their house and avoid getting completely foreclosed on.

Unfortunately, we're also seeing people wait too long to request a *Guaranteed Cash Offer* and lose out on hundreds of thousands of dollars in equity in these situations. Don't let this happen to you!

Bottom Line

In many cases, accepting your *Guaranteed Cash Offer* can help you avoid foreclosure, losing your house or having to execute a short sale. By giving you a fair and competitive offer and allowing you to keep the portion of the purchase price that would otherwise be lost to agent commissions and closing costs, it puts you in a better position. Accepting your *Guaranteed Cash Offer* can also help you if you're already in foreclosure, but you need to call us right away!

22. You have IVS: "Inflated Valuation Syndrome."

Most people assume that the house value they see on their property tax statement is accurate. They also check the estimated value online through places that provide those numbers for free.

ADDITIONAL RESOURCE!

Use our offer calculator to get your initial offer now without talking to a salesperson. Just scan the QR code below.

It's human nature to do these things. But how reliable are these numbers, and what happens when you take them as gospel when it's time to sell your house? You might fall into Inflated Valuation Syndrome, or IVS.

I see IVS more and more these days: Homeowners track their (supposed) property values online and through their property tax statements, then they list their house for that amount. If you do this, here's what you might not realize:

- Your county might be changing valuations to boost tax revenues.

- A lot of people buy houses based on school rankings and test scores, and you might not realize that your school district is changing, which will usually impact your home value.

- Finding the 10 most recent property sales in your neighborhood would give you much better intelligence about your property's true market value.

As a result, you might discover that the open market sees your house as overvalued by $100,000. Over the next few months, you may have to reduce your property's price multiple times. Big problem.

Real estate is local. A distant algorithm can't walk into your house and tell you what it's worth, and the county never does. The formulas they use don't know the nuances of repairs and updates. In fact, they might value two identical properties side by side at the same price, even when one has been completely updated and the other has mold in the basement and the kitchen it was built with in 1957.

If you suffer from IVS, you might find yourself in a risky situation: Your house is sitting on the open market. Consumers are seeing price reductions. Everyone's wondering, "What's wrong with that house?"

Accepting your *Guaranteed Cash Offer* avoids this problem. You receive a fair and competitive offer for your property. You take into account the time and money you save by *not* putting your house on the open market. And you simply say yes or no.

Bottom Line

Don't use online or government valuation tools to justify a value you want to sell your house for, because county and online property value estimates can come back to bite you. Accepting your *Guaranteed Cash Offer* avoids these pitfalls and guarantees that your property doesn't get stuck on the open market.

23. You've underestimated the cost of preparing your house.

If you run a business or a department within a company, then you know what a profit and loss statement is. Why don't we do a P&L when we sell our own house?

As a seller on the open market, you receive financial information from your agent and brokerage that may paint an incomplete picture and that no other business would accept. You learn the selling price, the commissions and fees, and that's basically it.

What's missing? Tons!

Do you know how much time you'll spend getting your house ready to sell on the open market? What's that time worth per hour? Do you know how much money you're going to spend on contractors and materials? How about those new curtains and bedspreads? Cleaning supplies? Landscaping? Staging?

If you don't have the resources to address these things, then accepting a *Guaranteed Cash Offer* might be an attractive option for you. The truth is, most people don't have the resources to cover the items listed in the middle column of the table at the end of this chapter.

But what happens if you start down the road of spending money to get your house ready, then run out of it? What if projects hit delays? If you need to sell quickly, this can be a major roadblock.

Selling on the open market puts you in the position of running a business for the first time in your life, and it can feel lonely and isolating. No one's there to train you on how to run the finances. No online calculator can accurately factor in every expense. There's no way to measure the money you're losing every extra day, week and month your house sits on the open market — let alone your loss of equity after five price reductions and the estimated commissions and closing costs of up to 10% that you could pay when you finally sell.

If these tools did exist, homeowners would learn the true cost of selling a house the old-fashioned way. And guess what? Many wouldn't do it.

Again, accepting your *Guaranteed Cash Offer* solves this problem. The entire process is transparent (more on this later), and you instantly know your true profit and loss. There are no commissions. No hidden fees. No lost money in time spent cleaning, decluttering and making repairs. No "days on market" factor. You automatically know what you're getting, and the offer costs you nothing.

Potential Expense List for Open-Market Selling vs. Accepting a *Guaranteed Cash Offer* on a $175,000–$400,000 House*

	Open-Market Home-Selling Expenses*	*Guaranteed Cash Offer* Expenses
Light Renovations (professional) (carpet, paint, fixtures, faucets)	$10,000–$20,000	$0
Major Renovations (professional) (furnace, A/C, roof, siding, windows, cabinets, flooring, electrical, plumbing, septic/well, driveway)	$30,000–$50,000	$0
Deep Cleaning	$200–$1,800	$0
Staging (accessories only)	$1,000–$1,500	$0
Staging (full furniture)	$3,000–$10,000	$0
Agent Commission (negotiable, but we often see 5%–8%)	$8,750–$32,000	$0
Seller Closing Costs (vary, but typically around 3%)	$5,250–$12,000	$0
Seller Paying Buyer Closing Costs (negotiable, up to 3%)	$5,250–$12,000	$0
Decluttering/Moving (depending on size of home and # of belongings)	$3,000–$10,000	$0
Holding Costs (assuming home is on market for 3 months)	$1,500–$3,000	$0
Price Reductions (if house stays on market too long; can be even more if market is declining)	$5,000–$20,000	$0
Repairs After Buyer Inspection	$1,000–$10,000	$0
Interest Rate Increase (e.g., rate jump of 1–2 percentage points while owner is getting the home ready to sell, triggering a price reduction)	$10,000–$20,000	$0
TOTAL	**$83,950–$202,300**	**$0**

* Numbers are estimated for many scenarios and can vary depending on the state, county or city where your property is located. Assumes the average sales price range for the market. A *Guaranteed Cash Offer* can apply to houses both above and below this value range.

Bottom Line

Sometimes you know up front that you don't have the resources to get your house ready to sell on the open market (often an additional 25% in expenses to make your property showroom-ready). Other times, you don't realize it until you're halfway through the process.

> **ADDITIONAL RESOURCE!**
>
> Use our offer calculator to get your initial offer now without talking to a salesperson. Just scan the QR code below.

Getting a *Guaranteed Cash Offer* costs you nothing. Accepting the offer gets you cash quickly, eliminates the extra costs of preparing your home, and saves valuable time and money. Simple.

24. You can't afford to fix current damages.

This one is related to the previous item, but it's worth its own mention. By "damages," I'm talking about any kind of destruction on your house: wind, hail or storm damage; family/tenant wear and tear; a noncompliant septic system or a failed water test ... the list goes on.

Most buyers aren't looking for a property that needs major work, but you might not have the money to make repairs. You also don't want to risk failing an inspection, and you might face other life situations that require you to move.

That's a lot of pressure.

Then add this: More and more insurers are pulling out of entire states (see: Florida, Minnesota and others) and creating carve-outs and exclusions. For example, home insurers used to have "matching" policies: If one side of your house got hit by hail and the insurer couldn't find siding to match the damaged side, then they'd pay to replace all four sides. Now they might only replace the damaged side, leaving you with mismatched siding and a lower property valuation.

So, do you have $50,000 sitting around to repair your house? If you don't, then it might be time to consider a *Guaranteed Cash Offer*. Buyers aren't looking for a total renovation project, and even if they are, they might not be able to secure a loan for it.

Accepting your *Guaranteed Cash Offer* sends you a lifeline. It's a fair offer that we believe reflects the current state of your house. We take on the cost and coordination of repairs. You're free to get on with your life.

Bottom Line

If your house has significant damages that you can't afford to fix, accepting your *Guaranteed Cash Offer* gets you out of a challenging situation. You have an instant buyer. You don't have to pay for repairs. And you can sell without worrying about failed inspections or buyer financing falling apart at the last minute.

25. You need more repairs and updates than you thought.

We already talked about the fact that the longer you live in a house, the less you notice how it smells. This is also true about how it looks: The longer you've lived in your house, the less you can see its quirks, imperfections and serious problems.

Want proof? Go into a few rooms and snap some pictures with your phone. Now look at them as if you were a homebuyer scanning an online listing. See those cracks in the drywall? Those out-of-date kitchen cabinets?

This is how others will see your property. If you can't afford to address those issues, then you should consider requesting a *Guaranteed Cash Offer*. If you *can* afford it, then you probably need to make a to-do list and start addressing each item soon.

Sometimes we reach a happy medium with a homeowner. If we see that their house needs a ton of work, we'll say, "Look, I can give you your *Guaranteed Cash Offer* later today. But I'm telling you right now, the market is going to put the offer closer to $190K, and it sounds like you were hoping for $350K. I don't want you to feel insulted, so maybe you do some of the work now to bring up that price. Whatever works for you."

Professional estimates almost always lead to sticker shock, so many homeowners try to fix things on their own. The problem is, buyers don't like it when repairs aren't professionally done, and neither do their home inspectors. If this happens to you, and your house fails an inspection or isn't up to code in certain areas, then you might spend even more money in the long run, or be stuck with faulty work you can't afford to fix.

If you're having a wake-up call about the true state of your house, then accepting a *Guaranteed Cash Offer* can be a real breath of fresh air. Skip the to-do list. Forget spending time and money on contractors. Don't DIY. It's not your problem. It's ours.

Bottom Line

If you don't work in real estate or remodel homes every day, you're probably going to significantly underestimate how many repairs and updates your house needs. I've seen too many homeowners not realize this until they're already in the process of selling on the open market. Don't risk it. Accept your *Guaranteed Cash Offer* instead, and let us deal with everything!

26. You had a buyer, but they backed out.

Say you list your house on the open market. Someone puts an offer on it. You accept it. Then the deal falls apart in the eleventh hour. Now you're back to square one.

Agents see this happen all the time, and it plays out way more often than you might think. Buyers who are going to live in your home are buying emotionally, so they're often finicky and uneasy. Maybe they don't like the inspection results. Maybe they have "buyer's remorse." Maybe they've lost their financing. Or maybe they've simply changed their minds.

If you thrive in unpredictable environments, then this risk might not bother you. You see it as part of the "open market" process, so accepting a *Guaranteed Cash Offer* isn't for you.

But think of all the things that could happen in the weeks and months after you start the open-market process all over again:

You could lose your job.

Your partner could lose their job.

You might have a contingency clause on your next house, and now you can't buy it.

The Feds might adjust interest rates.

The local or regional economy could plunge into recession.

A global conflict might drive down the stock market.

Accepting your *Guaranteed Cash Offer* erases these risks and puts you in control. We're rational buyers. Once you accept the offer, it's done. No one's going to change their mind, get cold feet or back out. You're shielded against external risks. So start packing!

Bottom Line

Human beings are unpredictable, and putting your house on the open market opens the door to emotional buyers. People who are going to live in your house are far more likely to demand last-minute changes that can slow the process, cause huge amounts of stress and create negative domino effects on your property sale. Accepting your *Guaranteed Cash Offer* keeps you in control. We're rational buyers, so you can make decisions with confidence. Choose when to close. Choose when to move. And choose a simpler, more predictable experience.

27. The age of your house has become a liability.

Anyone who's going to live in your house wants it to have a modern layout and be in perfect condition on day one. If your house has an old floor plan, you'll probably have a tough time selling it to a "move in" buyer.

But even if you do find a buyer, they may order a house inspection. And if your property is of a certain age, the inspector is usually going to find things wrong with it.

A worn roof. Broken shingles. Old appliances. Malfunctioning drain tile systems. Mechanical issues. Asbestos. Lead paint. Old (maybe original) windows. A dated kitchen and/or bathrooms. A noncompliant septic system or failed water test. Something that got damaged in the house and was never fixed.

The longer you own a property — especially an older house — the more big-ticket items likely need to be replaced (or you'll need to lower your asking price).

In my experience as a real estate agent and broker, I've seen many owners of older houses fail to see problems until they put their property on the open market. The don't realize how old the heating and air-conditioning systems are, or that the electrical is way out of date and not up to code. Sometimes we'll have a conversation that goes like this:

"How old is your roof?"
—*"It's new. We replaced it right after we bought the house 25 years ago."*

"I don't know how to tell you this, but that's not new."

Your property's expensive problems can quickly overshadow its old-world charms. Plus, you can find yourself shelling out thousands of dollars to buy modern systems and shiny new appliances for someone else.

Accepting your *Guaranteed Cash Offer* brings sanity (and savings) to this situation. You sell your house "as is." We take on the expense of replacing big-ticket items. You simply collect your check, choose your move date and move on.

Bottom Line

Putting an older house on the open market can mean spending tens of thousands of dollars to update the floor plan, install a new roof, replace old appliances, you name it. Do you have that kind of cash? Do you have the time to do the work? Accepting your *Guaranteed Cash Offer* lets you save the time, avoid the stress and steer clear of doing the work yourself.

28. You're stuck with a deadbeat rental property.

Let's look at four common challenges that can come up when you own one or more rental properties.

First, let's say you had a low-interest mortgage on a house (or no mortgage at all), then a life-changing event required you to move, and you turned the property into a rental. You've made a small profit over the years, but the current tenants have damaged the property and stopped paying rent.

Now you have to spend time and money getting it ready to rent or sell again, and you don't have either. You're also continuing to pay property taxes, as well as landscaping, insurance, water features, you name it.

To make matters worse, the problem tenants won't leave and aren't cooperating with showings. Houses don't show well when non-owners live there, especially when they don't take care of the property. The result: You can't find a buyer or a new renter.

The next one recently happened in a suburb near where I live. Say you have two properties: one you live in and another you've turned into a profitable rental. Or maybe you bought a bunch of rentals with little money down, hoping to build a local real estate empire.

Now the city passes an ordinance banning rentals, and you're stuck paying multiple mortgages with no tenants. What do you do?

If you put the properties on the open market, you'll probably spend a significant amount of time and money getting them ready to show. If they don't sell right away, you'll still be paying several months' worth of multiple mortgages.

In the third situation, you own a house and are able to pay your mortgage, but property values in your area are changing and aren't where they need to be for you to put it on the open market. You turn it into a rental instead.

Maybe you can't find tenants because people don't have the cash they used to have. Maybe you don't have the money to fix it up. Maybe you've found tenants, but you had to set the rent below market levels to get them and are losing money every month. Or maybe your tenants have stopped paying rent and have trashed the place to the tune of $50,000. Not only do you have to evict them, which could take months, but you'll also have to cover the mortgage and fix up the house to attract new tenants.

ADDITIONAL RESOURCE!

Has your city or municipality banned rentals? Find out by scanning the QR code below.

You could put the house on the open market, but you'll still need $50,000 for repairs. You'll be down for three months of mortgage payments. And if it doesn't sell, you could face the prospect of constant price reductions eroding your equity.

Lastly, maybe you've become an "accidental landlord": You never intended to manage a property, but for whatever reason, you needed to rent out a house you used to live in. You're "half in" on managing it because it's not a passion of yours, and you don't have enough rentals to bring in the profits needed to hire a professional property management company. Now the house has become a drain in more ways than one.

What do these three challenges have in common? Accepting a *Guaranteed Cash Offer* solves all of them. You don't need to cover the cost of damages. You don't need to fix up the house to attract new buyers or renters. All you have to do is accept your offer and leave the headaches to us.

Bottom Line

Rental properties can lead to complicated challenges with problem tenants. Accepting your *Guaranteed Cash Offer* frees you from paying for damages, getting a property ready for market or trying to conduct showings with tenants living in the house.

29. You have to pay off tax liens.

This is rare, but it does happen. Here's the situation:

If you're behind on your taxes, the IRS (or the state) can put liens on your property. The IRS always seems to be on the verge of hiring thousands of new auditors, so you never know when these actions could get more aggressive.

Tax liens mean the government has the right to keep possession of your property until your debt is paid. You can't sell it and pocket the equity until the lien debts are satisfied. Worse yet, the government can charge you interest and penalties. The longer liens sit, the more they eat into your equity. You can even have your wages garnished.

All of this points to one thing: You have to sell your house to pay the tax liens. Here's the problem: You can't hide the liens. They're discoverable during a title search, and they can cause serious problems in the financing process. Governments generally want liens to be paid off first. But banks want mortgages to take priority. And they can stop the mortgage approval process when they discover liens.

Translation: You can't attract a buyer because they might not be able to buy your house due to your tax liens.

When you accept your *Guaranteed Cash Offer*, you cut through these risks and uncertainties. Assuming your liens aren't so big that even a competitive offer won't pay them off, accepting your offer completely bypasses the mortgage lender/bank process. We're fully aware of the liens, and we're responsible for our own financing.

Bottom Line

Tax liens can make it nearly impossible to sell your house. When you put it on the open market, buyers might struggle to get financing from a bank or other mortgage lender. Accepting your *Guaranteed Cash Offer* frees you to sell your property, pay off your liens and keep moving forward.

"JUST TELL ME THE NUMBER" SYNDROME

THE FIVE WORDS that tell me a homeowner might not be right for a *Guaranteed Cash Offer* are "just tell me the number." Why? Because they don't realize that the "number" (the actual offer) is only part of the overall value a *Guaranteed Cash Offer* delivers.

If a homeowner "just wants the number," that usually means one of three things:

1) They're going to say the same thing to other acquisition companies, and they might accept the highest number while assuming that the company can get them to closing.

2) Their house has been struggling on the open market, and their real estate agent wants to change the listing price to match the *Guaranteed Cash Offer* number.

3) There's a number they're hoping to get, and they're going to wait until they get it.

In the first instance, you might be comparing apples to oranges. Do you want the ability to pick your closing date? Stay in the house after you close? Take advantage of additional time-saving services, like packing and moving? Take sentimental parts of the house with you? Then make sure your potential buyer offers those options — and that they have a positive track record in the industry.

You're also comparing apples to oranges in the second case. Why? Because an open-market house sale number is a *gross* number. Tons of fees are going to come out of it, including commissions, closing costs and inspection costs. When you accept your *Guaranteed Cash Offer*, you don't pay any of those fees. Plus, you gain the freedom to choose your closing and move-out dates, which gives you more time to find your next living situation.

In the third case, the homeowner might find an acquisition company that offers their preferred number. The question is, can they actually get to closing at that number?

Remember: The homeowner doesn't determine market value; the market does. That number is based on dozens of factors, including the condition of the property. If you're like most homeowners, your ideal number can't realistically happen. And the longer you fight for it, the less you'll likely make. I've seen too many situations where a homeowner could have done better if they'd taken their first *Guaranteed Cash Offer*. I don't want that to happen to you.

In short, "just give me the number" is a "tell." It tells me that you're a transactional person who's willing to spend a year haggling for an ideal number you may not get. If that's the case, then you might not be right (or ready) to accept a *Guaranteed Cash Offer*.

We're looking for people who understand the full value of what they're getting and are ready to start living the next chapter of their life.

IV. MINIMIZING RISK

SOME PEOPLE DON'T mind rolling the dice; others want to eliminate as much risk as possible when it comes to their biggest financial asset. In these scenarios, accepting your *Guaranteed Cash Offer* may relieve you of risks that you can't (or don't want to) deal with.

30. You want to avoid lawsuits.

Here's something that most first-time home-sellers don't know: If you put your house on the open market, you'll likely complete a disclosure form that basically says "this is everything I know about my house." You essentially give the buyer a warranty that says you're not hiding anything.

> **Open-Market Selling**
>
> Selling your house the old, slow way. Constantly negotiating. Hiring an agent. Arranging showings and open houses. And then paying commissions and closing costs.

Some homeowners think this frees them from future liabilities related to the house after it changes hands. It likely doesn't. The buyer can still call you a year later, accuse you of failure to disclose a problem and demand money from you. Even if you *did* properly disclose everything, you might have to pay to defend yourself. An arbitrator or court might decide that you're liable for lack of disclosure, so this scenario is filled with uncertainty.

Because it's an "as is" transaction, a *Guaranteed Cash Offer* lowers certain legal risks in selling your property. In a nutshell, you're more protected from surprises. You don't have to worry about a move-in buyer suing you or taking you to arbitration over a problem they find later. In general, if we find something in the house after our inspection and after we've purchased it, it's our problem, not yours.

Bottom Line

When you sell your house on the open market, you can still be held liable for problems after you've sold it. With a *Guaranteed Cash Offer*, "as is" means exactly that. Once you accept your offer and your property passes a routine inspection to rule out major problems, we assume responsibility for repairs and other issues.

31. You want to avoid emotional or unpredictable buyers.

We touched on this issue previously, but it's worth expanding here. When you expose yourself and your home to the open market, you enter an emotional and unpredictable world.

You're dealing with people who are buying your house to live in vs. a company that's likely going to fix it up and sell it, and there's a big difference!

I've been involved in thousands of transactions as an agent and broker. I've seen closings with emotional buyers fall apart, and I've seen every last-minute buyer request, demand and curveball you can imagine:

> *"We've fallen in love with your living room couch, so you need to leave it for us."*

> *"You need to refinish the basement. We walked down there, and our kids' allergies went crazy."*

> *"You need to remove everything from the house and hire an odor-removal company."*

Also, if you've never sold a house, or you haven't sold one for 20 years, don't be surprised when your agent calls and says, "I know we're supposed to close tomorrow, but one of the buyers just lost their job."

In addition to being volatility-proof, one of the greatest benefits of accepting your *Guaranteed Cash Offer* is that it's surprise- and emotion-proof. You're not dealing with an emotional buyer with a potential set of problems. You're dealing with a company, and we're not going to live in your house. We'll deal with the buyers so you don't have to.

Bottom Line

Emotions run high when you expose your house to the open market. The closer you get to your closing date, the more you might get left-field requests (or hear about unexpected turns of events) from the buyer. Accepting your *Guaranteed Cash Offer* removes emotions from the equation. No curveballs. Just one smooth transaction.

32. You don't like surprises from contractors.

Speaking of surprises, raise your hand if you've ever had a contractor tell you about a "new discovery" that's going to cost you more time and money than you expected. Now raise your hand if you don't love the idea of acting as a general contractor yourself, managing subcontractors and spending hours of your spare time every day holding them accountable.

That's a lot of hands.

Most property sales on the open market require some renovations and repairs. Which means they probably involve builders and contractors. Which means "surprises" are bound to pop up, and trust is likely to go down.

Could be structural issues. Could be electrical problems. Maybe the demolition team opened up a wall and discovered asbestos or mold. Maybe someone found lead-based paint. Now you need to abate the entire house, and it's going to cost $25,000 you don't have. Or the surprise could be any number of "delays": construction delays, contractor delays, remodeling delays, logjams in the drywall supply chain. Maybe your contractor just stopped showing up!

Most contractors are honest. They don't know what problems they're going to face until they start tearing things down. But inexperienced homeowners aren't used to this, and it can come as a shock. A very expensive shock.

Imagine selling your house because you're going through a divorce, and on top of all that stress, you have a growing list of problems with the contractor who's getting your house ready to sell. Sound like fun?

By eliminating the need for repairs and renovations on the open market, accepting your *Guaranteed Cash Offer* lets you avoid contractor surprises. It's that simple.

Bottom Line

Finding a team of contractors you trust is a huge challenge. And nothing is more common — or more annoying — than dealing with the never-ending number of "surprises" that come with any level of construction on your house. When you accept your *Guaranteed Cash Offer*, you free yourself from those surprises.

33. You want a hedge against economic volatility.

Change is the only constant, especially when it comes to the economy. Maybe this doesn't bother you. Maybe you're a natural gambler, and you're used to "rolling the dice" in many facets of your life. In that case, accepting a *Guaranteed Cash Offer* might not appeal to you.

But many people who sell their house on the open market start to sense that something doesn't feel right. Is the economy changing? Is the real estate market about to crash? Is my company struggling?

If you're in this position, you might also wonder:

Are real estate prices going to go up or down?

Are we in a bull market or a bear market, and when will that change?

Is unemployment rising or falling?

Is the Fed going to raise or lower interest rates, or keep them the same?

What are the levels of consumer savings and debt right now? How about student loan debt?

Don't forget the local concerns. How many other houses in your area are for sale? How many people are looking to buy? What are the current crime rates? Is your neighborhood getting safer or more dangerous? Are there enough jobs? Are wages in your area keeping up with inflation? Where are the buyers for your house going to come from? Do they have jobs and a steady paycheck?

You have to go to city and county law enforcement resources to do all this research on your own, and it can result in overwhelming confusion and uncertainty. And what if your research uncovers problems? You can have the greatest property in the world, but that doesn't matter if you can't find a buyer in the open market. The result: Your real estate agent might push you to keep dropping your asking price so they can earn their commission.

When you accept your *Guaranteed Cash Offer*, these constantly changing factors have little to no effect on your transaction. Stop trying to predict the future. Cut through the uncertainty instead, and feel confident about your decision.

Bottom Line

Putting your house on the open market exposes you to volatility. Accepting your *Guaranteed Cash Offer* is the volatility-proof way to sell.

34. You don't want to deal with emotional buyer inspections.

When you expose your house to the open market, emotional buyer inspections can cause a lot of anxiety — as well as tense negotiations.

As I've said before, if you're selling your house to someone who's going to live in it, they'll look hard for problems that will give them negotiating leverage. How will that affect you as the seller? Simple: You thought you were going to get a high purchase price. Now the buyer's agent is giving you a lowball offer.

Inspections are different in the *Guaranteed Cash Offer* world. You're not dealing with someone who's buying your house to live in. There's still an inspection, but it's less rigorous than an open-market buyer inspection. We just want to make sure there's nothing significantly wrong with your house, and we're happy to take on the smaller stuff ourselves.

Bottom Line

House inspections are often designed to give buyers more leverage so they can lower their offer. Inspections in the *Guaranteed Cash Offer* world are focused on uncovering major issues. We assume responsibility for the smaller ones, which means less risk and more peace of mind for you.

35. You want to avoid temporary housing and storage.

"We put our house on the market because we needed the equity to buy the next place. It sold fast, and now we can't find any place to go. Do we have to move in with family or friends?"

This can be a nightmare scenario, especially if you don't have friends or family to move in with. Where are you going to go?

Decent temporary housing isn't easy to find these days. Landlords don't want to constantly fix their places up and find new tenants because it eats into their profit margins. So why issue two-month leases when most tenants are willing to sign for a year?

The result: If your house sells before you find the next place to live, you'll likely pay a huge premium to secure temporary housing for a few months. And then there's your stuff. Where are you going to store it? Is your temporary space big enough, or will you need to rent storage? Who's going to handle the moving? Can you afford to rent a big enough truck?

Accepting your *Guaranteed Cash Offer* makes it easy to avoid temporary housing and storage hassles. Once you accept your offer, you pick your Cash Closing date. Do you have to move out on that date? No! If you need more time, we can work out an arrangement to help you stay put while you keep looking.

Bottom Line

If your house sells before you've found your next residence, you can be thrown into housing limbo. If you can't stay with a friend or family member, you'll pay a fortune for a hotel or other temporary housing and storage. When you accept your *Guaranteed Cash Offer*, you can close one day and move out later.

36. You want to avoid title issues.

Most people don't know what a title is or how it works. So when you hear, "Something came up on the title that wasn't detected when you bought your house," you have no idea what that means or the pain it's about to cause.

Here's the deal: Sometimes when you sell your house, you discover an old mortgage on it that never cleared. Paperwork wasn't digitized when you bought the place, so you don't have the information on your hard drive or in your email. Maybe you have an old paper folder with contact information for the title and mortgage companies, but guess what? They're both out of business!

Now you have a lien on your property that could take a year or more to fight. If you put it on the open market, you'll find that no bank is going to lend you money for your next house.

Accepting your *Guaranteed Cash Offer* is the easy solution to this problem. We usually take on the title issue. You can simply collect your cash and move on with your life.

Bottom Line

Title issues can dramatically complicate a property sale, especially if you discover that an old mortgage never cleared and the parties involved are out of business. Accepting your *Guaranteed Cash Offer* can take this risk off your plate.

37. You want to avoid a "race to the bottom."

I've touched on this in previous chapters, but let's really focus on it here.

The kiss of death when your house is on the open market is a "race to the bottom" where you're forced to lower your asking price multiple times to attract a buyer. This can happen in several ways.

Do you still have a mortgage on your house? Then you probably can't go below a certain asking price. What happens when you compete against other sellers in your area who've paid off their mortgages? They have more flexibility in their asking price, so you enter a race to the bottom to keep up.

ADDITIONAL RESOURCE!

Not ready to sell your house fast through a *Guaranteed Cash Offer*? Start with a home evaluation and find out what your house is worth by scanning the QR code.

What if you pick the wrong asking price from the start? If someone with a similar house in your area is more motivated to sell and chooses a more competitive asking price, then you'll face pressure to lower yours. As this pattern repeats itself, the profit on your property sale approaches zero. Even if you do sell, now you have to shell out commissions and closing costs.

What if you feel like your neighborhood is getting less desirable, or that something big — locally or in the world — has changed or is about to change? I've seen plenty of situations where people in an area start to "panic sell," triggering a race to the bottom in property values.

Finally, what if buyers simply aren't shopping in your area? Properties, including yours, could sit on the market for days, weeks, months. As we've talked about before, the higher your "days on market" number is, the more buyers will start to think "what's wrong with that house?" and stay away.

Accepting your *Guaranteed Cash Offer* keeps you out of these races to the bottom. Your house is never listed. It's not subject to downward price pressures. You don't have to chase the market with constant showings to find buyers. You receive a fair and competitive offer. All you have to do is say yes.

Bottom Line

Many scenarios can create a "race to the bottom" when it comes to property values in your area, forcing you to lower your asking price and enter a price war you can't win. Plus, they can create a pricing history online for your house that will never go away. Accepting your *Guaranteed Cash Offer* saves you from constant price cuts and guarantees that your house will sell.

38. Preparing your house won't be safe for you or your partner.

Concussions. Puncture wounds from nails and other sharp objects. Broken bones from roof and ladder falls. Contusions, abrasions and lacerations from saws, hammers and other power tools. Thrown-out backs from lifting heavy items during decluttering. I've seen them all.

Once you expose your house to the open market and commit to winning the online beauty contest, you risk injury by making dozens of repairs and updates — especially as you age. Are you ready for that?

Even if you or your partner is handy, these projects might be too much to take on. Maybe it's your age. Maybe one of you has a medical condition that limits your physical abilities. If one of you wants to try the open market and the other doesn't, that only adds to the tension.

If a doctor warns against ladders and steps, you'll have to hire professionals to do the work. Can you afford to hire contractors? Do you have the time to manage them? What if their work doesn't meet your standards, or they don't get the job done on time and on budget?

Accepting your *Guaranteed Cash Offer* wipes away all these concerns. With no repairs to make, no furniture or appliances to move and no contractors to manage, you can focus on the two things that matter most: your health and finding your next residence.

Bottom Line

Putting your house on the open market exposes you and your partner to potentially dangerous repairs and renovations. Are you physically and mentally capable of an hour of hard labor, let alone hundreds? If not, are you up to the task of managing half a dozen contractors? Accepting your *Guaranteed Cash Offer* frees you from the physical labor required to get it ready.

39. You might face costly and disruptive code violations.

As a seller, you want to avoid surprises, but you can get a lot of them after a city inspection on your house. Here's what I mean:

Say your property's previous owners did a lot of DIY work on it. Maybe they added a master bedroom on the top floor. Maybe they put a bathroom on the main floor or finished the basement. Many cities require an inspection before you sell. Other times you might want one so you can know what the city (and the buyer's inspector) might find later on.

After the city inspection, you might hear things like "the plumbing in that new bathroom isn't up to code," "you have a noncompliant septic system" or "we can't find permits for the electrical work." Now you have to hire contractors and spend $30K–$100K that was supposed to go toward a down payment on your next house. Do you have that kind of money? Even if you do, will the investment pay off?

These findings may also be red flags you have to disclose to an emotional buyer in the open market, which might affect their financing and derail a sale.

Accepting your *Guaranteed Cash Offer* solves this by freeing you from correcting code violations and permit problems, or from having to redo any work yourself. Like the title, the headaches transfer from you to us.

Bottom Line

Your house might be filled with code violations and other problems that you won't know about until the city inspects it. Do you have the time and money to fix these issues? When you accept your *Guaranteed Cash Offer*, it's our problem, not yours.

40. You have potentially high holding costs.

Also called "carrying costs," holding costs refer to the expenses involved in holding (owning) a property before a new owner takes possession of it after an open-market sale. This includes the mortgage, but it also includes property taxes, escrow, insurance, utilities, lines of credit, property management and neglected maintenance.

> **Open-Market Selling**
>
> Selling your house the old, slow way. Constantly negotiating. Hiring an agent. Arranging showings and open houses. And then paying commissions and closing costs.

Additional holding costs are seasonal and become more expensive the more the weather varies in your area. These might include landscaping, pools, water features and sprinkler systems. Some of these expenses go up in spring and summer. If your house hasn't sold by late autumn and you live in a cold climate, you have holding costs involved in shutting things down for the winter.

When you expose your house to the open market, you may have no idea how long you'll have to keep paying holding costs. Could be weeks, could be months, and that adds up quickly. If you've already bought another property or secured a rental, co-op or assisted-living residence, the costs could go even higher.

When you accept your *Guaranteed Cash Offer*, you pick your Cash Closing date. You know exactly what you're going to pay in holding costs, and it's almost certainly thousands of dollars less than what you would pay if you put your house on the open market. Plus, you avoid paying commissions.

Bottom Line

Most people don't consider holding costs when they put their house on the open market, and some aren't prepared to fork over the money to keep the property maintained through different seasons. By letting you pick your closing date, accepting your *Guaranteed Cash Offer* dramatically limits your holding costs. You know exactly what you need to do, when you need to do it and how much it's going to cost.

41. You don't want to sell a vacant house.

An unstaged house looks worse than a staged one online, and a vacant property can be even less appealing on the open market. Empty space doesn't leave more to the buyer's imagination. It makes your house look uninviting. If you try to sell your vacant house on the open market, it won't show as well and will likely result in fewer and lower bids, or no bids at all.

Sometimes you don't have a choice. Maybe you're selling a property that you don't currently live in. Maybe your house got flooded. Or maybe you've had to move your furniture into storage or a new residence due to a job relocation or other life event.

If you put your house on the open market in these scenarios, you start at a huge disadvantage. First, there's the potential damage (water, ice dams, roof leaks, etc.) that can happen without you even knowing about it. Second, people who are going to live in your home are emotional buyers, so it's all about how they feel when they see your house. You might have the best property available in your area, but it won't attract the same interest as the ones that are properly staged. Even if you digitally stage your property, word will spread that the online impression is deceiving.

Accepting your *Guaranteed Cash Offer* gives you a different option for these situations. You don't have to worry about how your house will look online or during a showing. In fact, a vacant property makes our job easier!

Bottom Line

A vacant house puts you at a disadvantage when you put your house on the open market. In addition to damages potentially happening without your knowledge, you won't attract the same buyer interest online as furnished and properly staged properties. If you're selling a vacant house or moving in a hurry and need everything out fast, accepting your *Guaranteed Cash Offer* can be a great way to streamline the process and avoid these risks.

42. You want to avoid "Contingency Limbo."

This one is pretty straightforward, and it's related to the timing issue we already talked about. As many as three out of every four properties sold on the open market have a contingency attached.[5] As a seller, that potentially throws you into Contingency Limbo: If you put your house on the open market and any part of the sale falls apart, you lose leverage and find yourself at the mercy of factors beyond your control.

Accepting your *Guaranteed Cash Offer* delivers far more certainty and far less risk when it comes to contingencies. You can have confidence that you'll sell your house, get your cash fast and avoid paying commissions.

After that, simply pick your Cash Closing date. Bank your proceeds. Pick your move date. Figure out what you can afford in your next residence. And buy it based on how well it fits your needs, not whether you can time it to the sale of your previous house.

Bottom Line

When you expose yourself and your house to the open market, contingency scenarios can cause high stress and sleepless nights. Accepting your *Guaranteed Cash Offer* helps you avoid

---

[5] https://www.krislindahl.com/books/guaranteed-cash-offer-book-notes/

Contingency Limbo because *you* have far more control over when you sell, close on and move out of your property.

43. You want to avoid "Days on Market Disease."

This one is related to the "race to the bottom" problem on the open market we've already discussed, and I can't tell you how many times I've seen it play out.

Have you ever driven through a residential area and seen open-house signs for a property everywhere, but no cars parked outside the house that's having it? There's a good chance that property is suffering from Days on Market Disease.

Say you're selling your house on the open market, and it has to list at a certain price to deliver the proceeds you want. You list it, and it doesn't sell in the first seven days. No big deal, right?

Not so fast. Let's say five more properties enter the market in your neighborhood. They're priced below yours, but you don't want to enter the "race to the bottom." You hold steady. The other properties sell, and buyer interest in yours dries up. The open houses aren't working. The showings are few and far between. The "days on market" number keeps climbing.

What happens now? The kiss of death. Buyers wonder what's wrong with your house, and the stigma won't go away. Technically, you can take it off the market and put it back on later, but today's buyers are too sophisticated and connected online to fall for that. Fact is, when you expose your house to the open market, its pricing history never goes away. Every potential buyer will be able to see it.

The more days, weeks and months that go by, the higher the pressure grows. If you've never sold a house before, I can't emphasize enough how much the day-to-day stress can consume you.

Accepting your *Guaranteed Cash Offer* lets you avoid Days on Market Disease and the anxiety that comes with it. You pick your Cash Closing date. We work together on a move-out date. Your house is never on the open market.

Bottom Line

If similar houses in your area list for lower than yours, and you don't cut your asking price, then you might be faced with Days on Market Disease. The longer your property stays on the open market, the less appealing it can become to buyers, and the more you might start to feel like your back is against the wall. Accepting your *Guaranteed Cash Offer* prevents Days on Market Disease. It sells quickly. You choose when to close and when to move. Boom, done!

V. PERSONALITY TRAITS

DO YOU HAVE THE right personality to accept a *Guaranteed Cash Offer*? Read this section to find out. While some people enjoy the dozens of tasks and hundreds of decisions involved in putting their house on the open market, most don't. Accepting your *Guaranteed Cash Offer* may fit your personality, if …

44. You don't like negotiations, let alone paying fees and commissions.

In my years as a real estate agent, I've sat across the kitchen table from thousands of people trying to sell their house. Depending on their personality, one issue rises to the top as their least-favorite part of the open-market selling process: *negotiations*.

In the open-market process, negotiations start with choosing an agent and don't end until your sale is closed with a move-in buyer. What does that mean? Constant uncertainty. Fear of things falling apart. Insecurity about being perceived as "stubborn" or "unreasonable." A nagging feeling of helplessness.

There's a reason why so many car dealerships and auto manufacturers have moved from a "haggling" model to offering "one fair price." Most people hate the bargaining process. It's the same reason why some jewelers emphasize the fact that they have non-commissioned salespeople. The implication is that you *won't have to negotiate*, and people like that.

So many property owners assume they'll only have to go through negotiations once when they sell on the open market. This is rare, especially in an uncertain economy and housing industry. In my experience, you're more likely to feel like you're endlessly negotiating.

You might interview an agent and negotiate commissions with them, then have to go through the entire process again to find a new agent when the market rejects your home. Same with buyers. You might jump through hoops to finally reach an agreement, then see it fall apart after you've already popped the champagne on a (supposed) deal. Again, you have to start over.

Even if you do survive the negotiating phase, will you be thrilled to pay commissions and closing costs? As I've mentioned in previous chapters, putting your house on the open market means you can likely expect to spend about 10% of the sale price or more on these costs, plus title fees, state deed taxes and other miscellaneous fees.

That's a big chunk of change, likely tens of thousands of dollars! Add it to the money you'll probably have to spend on repairs, renovations and other updates — assuming you even have that kind of money — and you can see why my companies deliver so many *Guaranteed Cash Offers* and are constantly buying homes.

Do you have to engage in negotiations in a *Guaranteed Cash Offer* sale? Nope! How many fees and commissions do you have to pay? None. Zero. Zilch. What you see is literally what you get. One fair offer. No bartering. No surprises.

Bottom Line

Are you the type of person who loves to haggle and go through the stress and uncertainty of endless negotiations? Even if the answer is yes, are you then okay with paying up to 10% of your home equity in commissions and fees once you've finally reached an agreement? If not, then accepting a *Guaranteed Cash Offer* might be a good fit for you. It's one fair number. All-inclusive and transparent. No negotiations. No commissions. No fees. No surprises.

45. You're risk-averse.

Let's talk more about risk. Before you expose yourself and your house to the open market, ask yourself, "What's my overall risk tolerance?" Because as you've seen, the open market exposes you to dozens of potential uncertainties:

- You might have to keep cutting your asking price.

- You might learn that you need tens of thousands of dollars in updates and repairs, and you don't have that kind of money.

- You might do a ton of work on your house only to find out that it was all wasted because consumer tastes have changed.

- An emotional buyer might change their mind and back out at the last minute.

- You might injure yourself trying to DIY repairs and renovations.

- In extreme cases, someone might steal the photos of your house they see online, advertise your property for sale or rent on other websites, and trick potential buyers and renters into wiring them money.

And on and on.

In my career as an agent and broker, I've talked to too many homeowners who've put their house on the open market, couldn't sell it, fired their real estate agent for another one, then went through the exact same pattern all over again.

> **Open-Market Selling**
>
> Selling your house the old, slow way. Constantly negotiating. Hiring an agent. Arranging showings and open houses. And then paying commissions and closing costs.

They lost significant time and money, especially in holding costs. And they might have been much better off if they had simply accepted our *Guaranteed Cash Offer*.

If your risk tolerance is high, feel free to go on the open market. But if you feel anxiety around selling your property, then you may not want to take on any added risks. Accepting your *Guaranteed Cash Offer* can lower your stress.

Bottom Line

Some people are gamblers with a high tolerance for risk. Most aren't. Exposing your house to the open market carries risks, from never-ending price reductions, to changes in interest rates that affect open-market buyers, to emotional buyers backing out at the last minute. By eliminating uncertainties, accepting a *Guaranteed Cash Offer* removes these risks and can lower your stress.

46. You don't like others dictating your schedule.

When I ask people to name their least favorite part of putting their house on the open market, I often hear something like this:

> *"I hated getting that alert telling me a showing was scheduled and I had minutes to leave the house and find something to do for the next hour."*

When you put your house on the open market, you lose control over your schedule. Buyers literally tell you when to leave. In the middle of dinner? It doesn't matter. You can decline a showing, but it works against you. You pretty much have to say yes, and it's a pain.

A selling process that was designed for agents can make you feel like a receptionist. *Ding! Another showing request. Time to go!* If you have a family (and pets), the process becomes even more inconvenient.

You may also have to be tech-savvy, responding to text messages and using new apps to respond to showing requests. Selling on the open market means you (or your parent or grandparent) might have to be on the phone nonstop.

A *Guaranteed Cash Offer* is designed around *you*. It's about *your* schedule. *Your* convenience. *Your* time. If you're the type of person who likes to be in control instead of at the mercy of other people's schedules, it might be the better way to go.

Bottom Line

Among all the inconveniences of exposing your property to the open market, few rank as high as leaving for showings at a moment's notice to let strangers inside your house. No one likes having their schedule dictated by other people. With no showings or open houses, accepting your *Guaranteed Cash Offer* keeps you in control.

47. You generally like to avoid conflict.

Let's face it: Some people thrive on conflict and others will do anything to avoid it. If you don't have a sentimental bone in your body, you enjoy managing people and projects, and you love being constantly presented with new problems to solve, then accepting a *Guaranteed Cash Offer* isn't for you.

But if you tend to avoid pain and conflict, let's talk. Because

ADDITIONAL RESOURCE!

Are you conflict-averse? Find out by scanning the QR code below.

sometimes the people who need to sell their house are the ones who most avoid doing it, just as they avoid tackling other stressful things in life. We all do it!

In my career as an agent and broker, I've worked with thousands of people who've regretted selling and buying houses on the open market because they didn't realize how many conflicts the process would create, especially with contractors.

I've seen countless others avoid the emotions of selling altogether. "This is where we raised our kids," they'll say. "This is where we spent every holiday for 20 years. We can't leave!" Others think their house is decluttered and ready for the open market when they've actually acquired more stuff and are further away. Emotionally, they're not ready to leave.

It's understandable. No one wants to feel like life is moving on without them, that they're losing control or (not to be morbid) that they're one step closer to the grave. But most people who avoid selling their house do so because they know how much conflict is involved. They've seen friends and family argue with contractors and haggle with buyers. They're so tired at the end of each day, the last thing they want to do is fight.

If this sounds familiar, then accepting *Guaranteed Cash Offer* is right for you. By avoiding a slew of interpersonal relationships, it makes the selling process faster, easier, smoother and more peaceful.

Bottom Line

If you tend to avoid conflict, then you're probably stuck when it comes to selling your house because you can't stop thinking about all the people you'll have to deal with in the process. Accepting your *Guaranteed Cash Offer* transforms an overwhelming experience into something that feels easy and conflict-free.

48. You value transparency.

Who are these strangers in my house? Do I trust them in my house without me there? Are they going to look through all my personal stuff? Who's the buyer's agent, and do they have any experience? What's the appraiser going to do? Why are these contractors here? What am I supposed to be doing next? Why won't anyone tell me anything?!

Until you sell your first house, you don't realize how much guesswork and anxiety are involved. From the moment you put it on the open market, you're constantly trying to see through a fog and figure out what buyers and their agents are doing and thinking.

In a lot of cases, you don't know and have never heard of the buyer's agent. Agents earn their licenses every day. If they're new, they might have no idea what they're doing or how to keep their buyers from doing anything they want.

If *you* have an inexperienced or less-skilled agent, you also might discover a bunch of hidden fees late in the process. Tons of people have told me about arriving at their closing and — even though their property's condition hasn't changed and they've paid their commissions and closing costs — hearing that they need to go back and bring a check for thousands of dollars more.

How would that sit with you?

When you accept your *Guaranteed Cash Offer*, everything is up front and out in the open. It's simple: Here are the numbers. Sign here. You're done. No appraisal, inspection or other hidden costs. It might be the most transparent transaction you'll ever complete.

Bottom Line

Putting your home on the open market can be a foggy process full of guesswork. If you don't like commissions and you value transparency, you'll appreciate the simplicity and straightforward nature of accepting your *Guaranteed Cash Offer*.

49. You like to save time and cut through the red tape.

Are you the kind of person who enjoys spending time on things you have no experience doing (or have never done before)? Few people are, and that's understandable. Unfortunately, completing the sale of a house on the open market can take months. According to a Realtor.com report, about 2 out of every 5 people say it took longer than they expected.[6]

Then there's the red tape. Exposing your house to the open market can involve enough of it to cover the globe with it three times over. Who doesn't remember closing on their first house and seeing that mountain of paperwork on the table?

---

[6] https://www.krislindahl.com/books/guaranteed-cash-offer-book-notes/

I often hear people joke that the three most stressful things in life are death, divorce and selling your house on the open market. Turns out it's true. One study cited on cnbc.com found that nearly 40% of people burst into tears at some point from the stress of it all.[7]

A huge reason for the time suck and tears is the number of players involved in the old-fashioned open-market process: agents, lenders, appraisers, inspectors, stagers, photographers, general contractors, subcontractors, plumbers, electricians, landscapers, strangers and nosy neighbors showing up for open houses. The list is never-ending.

Each of these groups represents another part of an overly complicated system. Another project to manage. Another person who might disappoint you or let you down. Another area where something could go wrong. More hours spent doing something you don't enjoy.

Accepting your *Guaranteed Cash Offer* cuts through that clutter and typically saves you hundreds of hours of time. You get an offer on the same day we visit your house. And when you transfer ownership to us, you also transfer the bureaucracy, hassles and headaches. In return, you get a fast process designed to respect every second of your time.

Bottom Line

Are you a patient person when it comes to bureaucracy and red tape? Putting your house on the open market involves players, projects and paperwork that can completely take over

---

[7] https://www.krislindahl.com/books/guaranteed-cash-offer-book-notes/

your life. Selling the *Guaranteed Cash Offer* way cuts through the red tape and gives you life's most precious commodity: time.

50. You value your sleep.

You might think I'm kidding with this one, but I'm not. Over the course of my career, people have confided in me about how poorly they slept while their house sat on the open market — to the point where it seriously impacted their health.

And why *wouldn't* you have trouble sleeping in that situation? When you expose yourself to the open market, your biggest investment sits there hoping to attract a buyer. You've invested a huge amount of time and money getting it showroom-ready for people with sky-high expectations. You're struggling to keep everything clean and perfect for showings. And you never know when you'll be forced to pack up the family and leave.

The uncertainty of the open market can cause an anxiety that starts to feed off itself. By contrast, accepting your *Guaranteed Cash Offer* puts your mind, body and soul at peace. One offer. One acceptance. No surprises. No anxiety.

Zzzzz …

Bottom Line

Selling your house isn't worth losing sleep over, yet that's exactly what happens when people expose their property to the open market and subject themselves to a world of volatility, uncertainty and risk. By being fast, convenient and predictable, a *Guaranteed Cash Offer* sale lets you sleep soundly at night.

51. You're nostalgic about your house.

The anxiety I just described often pushes homeowners into a paralyzing state of nostalgia. "Why am I subjecting myself to all this stress?" they ask themselves. "I love this house, and I'll miss it if I sell it. I'm taking it off the market!"

Maybe this describes you, or maybe you haven't sold your property yet because you can't stop thinking about all the things you'll miss. Logically, you know it's best to sell. Emotionally, you (or your partner) can't bring yourself to do it.

Nostalgia can't be cured. Houses are emotional places. It's hard to say goodbye to the first property you and your partner bought, the room where your daughter practiced the piano, the backyard where you and your son played catch.

I've learned that many people need to take their houses with them in some way, especially if they raised a family there. Maybe it's having a local artist paint a picture of it. Maybe it's having a professional photographer capture it in its best season. The point is to have your memories travel with you.

Sometimes we include these items in a *Guaranteed Cash Offer*. Even more importantly, we make it easy for you to take a sentimental part of your house with you. Maybe you love a certain door, and you want to have it in the next house as well. An open-market buyer might refuse to let you take it.

As a *Guaranteed Cash Offer* buyer, my companies don't have the same emotional attachments as people who are going to actually live in your house. It's about *you*, not us. We understand your nostalgia, so take that door with you!

Bottom Line

Are you sentimental about your house? Nostalgia doesn't have to get in the way of selling it. While putting your house on the open market severely limits your options to "take a piece of it with you," accepting your *Guaranteed Cash Offer* gives you more choices. We can help you obtain a high-quality painting or photo of your house. And if you want to take a part of it with you — a favorite door or mirror — we're far more likely than an open-market buyer to let you do it. So leave the stress and hassles behind, and bring the memories with you!

52. You don't like being tied down or locked into anything.

How do you feel about others restricting your freedoms and dictating your choices in life? If that's not your thing, then you should know that when you put your house on the open market, you can find yourself locked into a long-term listing contract that limits your options and likely includes big commissions you're supposed to pay.

If you don't like feeling "tied down," then accepting your *Guaranteed Cash Offer* may be the way to go. You receive your offer on the same day we visit your house, and you're under no obligation to accept it. It's a simple, no-haggle offer: "Here's the number. You can agree to it, or you can walk away, no questions asked."

I structured it that way because *I* don't like being tied down and having my freedoms limited, and I'm guessing you don't either. Accepting your *Guaranteed Cash Offer* gives you a fast, easy and convenient way to sell your house. No listing contracts means more freedom.

Bottom Line

Putting your house on the open market often starts with locking yourself into a long-term listing contract that includes commissions for your agent. When you get a *Guaranteed Cash Offer* on your house, you're under no obligation to accept it, and you pay no commissions.

VI. PRIVACY

FINALLY, LET'S TALK about something we all value: privacy. Your home is an intimate space that reflects who you are. There's a reason you don't let just anyone walk inside. Yet putting your house on the open market literally flings the doors open to any stranger off the street. Let's conclude these scenarios by talking about some of the reasons why people accept a *Guaranteed Cash Offer* to protect and preserve their privacy.

53. You don't like having strangers in your house.

When I tell people who've never sold a house that one of the top benefits of accepting a *Guaranteed Cash Offer* is "discretion," they're surprised. I mentioned this in the chapter about sellers going through a divorce, and it's worth talking about here as well.

When you expose your house to the open market, you thrust everything into full public view. Photos of your personal space go online for everyone to see. Everybody knows your house is for sale, how much you're asking for it and how long it's been on the market. Anyone can scrutinize every nook and cranny. If you're sensitive about your health or immunocompromised, you'll probably think constantly about the germs being left in your house every day.

In addition, any stranger can walk through your front door without a background check or reference, and without being preapproved. You'd be surprised how many tire-kickers come out of the woodwork to walk through a house that's for sale on the open market, which only wastes time and adds to your inconvenience.

In some tight-knit neighborhoods, this whole process leads to gossip.

Did he lose his job?

I heard they're separating.

Really? I heard it was a gambling issue.

I heard she has a health issue.

In addition to random people walking through your property and potentially getting into your stuff, you have nosy neighbors going to your open houses and whispering their judgments to each other.

Did you see how they lived? OMG those decorating choices!

Can you believe how much stuff they have?!

Why wouldn't you change that wallpaper?!

Can you believe they haven't replaced those kitchen cabinets?

Accepting your *Guaranteed Cash Offer* keeps everything private and everyone out of your house. Strangers don't see photos showing the actual interior condition of your (or a relative's) intimate space. There's never a lockbox on the door handle or a sign in the front yard screaming *There's something going on here!* to

> ## Open-Market Selling
>
> Selling your house the old, slow way. Constantly negotiating. Hiring an agent. Arranging showings and open houses. And then paying commissions and closing costs.

the neighbors. No one gets to walk around your private space and get into your private business.

In short, accepting your *Guaranteed Cash Offer* keeps your doors locked, your valuables safe and your house sale a secret. You decide who knows what and who gets to enter. The neighbors don't know what's going on until you've moved out.

Bottom Line

Most people want their house sale to be a private matter. But when you expose it to the open market, everybody knows what's happening, and you have to trust strangers to respect your house and not tamper with your personal items. After speed and convenience, the most prized benefits of accepting your *Guaranteed Cash Offer* are discretion and secrecy. Don't underestimate them!

54. You don't want to offend an agent friend.

Don't laugh — this one is HUGE!

On the open market, the stakes are high in hiring a real estate agent. You can lose a lot of money if you go with one who lacks knowledge or has the wrong marketing strategy.

A better approach might be to explore your *Guaranteed Cash Offer* options before ever talking to a real estate agent. Their interests aren't necessarily yours. They'll likely try to convince you to hire them and go the stressful open-market route so they can earn a commission.

But saying no isn't always easy to do. Because if you're like most people, you know at least five real estate agents, many of whom do it part time. Could be your sister, your nephew, your neighbor, a server at your favorite restaurant, a younger relative's soccer coach.

At some point, these people have handed you their business card and told you to contact them when it's time to sell your house. They like you and want to help you, but let's be honest: They also want that commission.

So what happens when you *do* subject your house to open-market forces? Everything goes public. A sign appears in the yard. The listing goes live all over the internet. And everyone sees which agent and brokerage you chose to work with.

What's it going to be like the next time you go to your relative's soccer game, host a holiday gathering or attend a neighborhood block party? That next trip to your favorite restaurant is going to be *aaawkward*!

When you accept your *Guaranteed Cash Offer*, you don't have to hire a real estate agent. That means you never have to interview anyone, think of the right questions to ask, wonder if they're going to be stretched thin by working with too many other sellers, or worry about hurting someone's feelings when you reject them.

In short, you'll never have to risk betting on the wrong person to sell your most important asset. The truth is, in most cases you know that going with your friend in an open-market strategy isn't going to work well. When you accept your *Guaranteed Cash Offer*, you get to skip all of it. Plus, it's an easy conversation to have after you've already closed and moved.

> *"Why didn't you hire me?"*
> —*"I didn't want to risk selling my house on the open market!"*

Bottom Line

Want to avoid awkward encounters with your friends, family members and colleagues who are real estate agents? Accepting your *Guaranteed Cash Offer* eliminates the need to even have an agent, so you won't offend anyone by not choosing them.

55. You don't like being judged.

Bet that one got your attention!

Here's the deal: When you put your house on the open market, it has to be photographed inside and out, and you have to allow showings that are open to the public. This is where the judgment comes in.

Online shoppers will judge you and your house based on the photos they see online. And after each showing, you'll see feedback collected by your agent from potential buyers and nosy neighbors.

Countless sellers have told me how deflated they've felt after reading negative buyer comments. They spent six months getting their house ready for the open market. They were excited for people to see it. Now they're reading things like "How did those people live in this cluttered dump?!"

Buyers can be like trolls on the internet. Their comments are anonymous, so some feel emboldened. They'll criticize your decorating. They'll slam your choice of cabinets, paints, tiles. They'll question how you could have lived in "such a cramped and trashy space for over 20 years." They'll basically tell you that the property you've put so much love into is a piece of crap.

Some sellers lose their confidence and never recover from this.

When you accept your *Guaranteed Cash Offer*, your house becomes a judgment-free zone. You don't subject it to the open market. You never have a showing or open house. And you won't be judged by people you've never met.

Bottom Line

If you're going to expose yourself and your house to the open market, you'd better have thick skin. Potential buyers can rip your house — and by extension, *you* — to shreds. Accepting your *Guaranteed Cash Offer* bypasses showings, allowing you to steer clear of obnoxious trolls and hurtful comments. Leave that to social media.

IN CONCLUSION: IT'S TIME TO ACCEPT YOUR *GUARANTEED CASH OFFER*!

CONGRATULATIONS! You've now probably read more about selling a house in the modern age than most of your friends, family and neighbors. Which means you should now feel confident in considering a *Guaranteed Cash Offer*.

After reading this book, can you see why so many people are going the *Guaranteed Cash Offer* route instead of paying commissions and dealing with the stresses of the slow and unpredictable open market?

As the founder of the *Guaranteed Cash Offer* program, I'm here to give you a breath of fresh air. Because I believe that when you accept your *Guaranteed Cash Offer*, you'll replace uncertainty with control, and replace stress with relief.

Whether you're about to close on your home with your *Guaranteed Cash Offer*, or you're standing by a loved one who's embarking on this journey, the peace of mind I hope you'll feel after closing is exactly why I crafted this quick, simple and straightforward house-selling program. That "I'm totally stressed out and overwhelmed" feeling that's been weighing you down? It's going to lift.

You may have noticed more and more companies in your area mimicking the *Guaranteed Cash Offer* program. They're doing that because countless homeowners have embraced our system and entered their next great adventure in life with ease and speed. These programs are imitations, not the real thing. And they may not be committed to giving you a fair and competitive offer or understanding your unique situation.

The *Guaranteed Cash Offer* program is more than a way to sell your house. It's an empowered community of people who have stepped confidently into a future unburdened by the past.

If you find yourself in a situation like the ones described in this book, hopefully you'll feel free to request a *Guaranteed Cash Offer* and ultimately make the decision that's right for you.

In closing …

> *Now that you've read this book, you might be more curious than ever about selling a house using a Guaranteed Cash Offer. You can apply for your no-obligation offer right now by simply filling out a quick application after scanning the QR code that follows.*

If you've already accepted your Guaranteed Cash Offer, congratulations and welcome to the community of others like you who've decided to be smart sellers! Thank you for trusting us, and we look forward to working with you.

Thanks again for reading this book. We look forward to closing your *Guaranteed Cash Offer* when it's right and convenient for you, and we're excited for you to feel the experience of selling the fast and easy way.

SCAN NOW!

Take a deep breath and feel the relief. Your big worries are about to get much smaller!

— Kris Lindahl

ACKNOWLEDGMENTS

TO THE ENTIRE Kris Lindahl Real Estate team, because none of this exists without each and every one of you. We started as a small underdog company determined to bring innovation and empathy to real estate. Today, we're globally recognized as an industry innovator that's never lost its local touch.

We've accomplished this evolution by staying committed. Staying focused. And staying a proud, independent brokerage obsessed with serving the amazing people and families in the communities where we live and work. Because of that, we've earned thousands of five-star reviews on Google and other major review sites.

Thank you for your hard work and commitment. Together, we've changed the real estate industry forever. The best part is, we'll continue to do so!

A special thank-you to my dear friend Marc for turning my thoughts and visions into a book that's going to help so many homeowners sell fast and stress-free!

WHAT DO I DO NEXT?
A SPECIAL OFFER

NOW THAT YOU'VE finished this book, I've got great news for you! When you call

1-855-967-SOLD

(1-855-967-7653)

or go to

GuaranteedCashOfferBook.com

you can receive everything on the next page
with our compliments:

- The ebook companion to this book, *The Smart Way to Handle an Aging Relative's Home.*

- Access to our brand-new *Guaranteed Cash Offer* calculator, which we created for people who need to get started on our program by receiving an instant offer.

- A video where I take a deeper dive into advanced *Guaranteed Cash Offer* strategies that will help you get MORE.

- My checklist: "The Stress-Free Guide to Maximizing Your Guaranteed Cash Offer."

- My handbook: *Kris Lindahl's Step-by-Step Guide to Making Your Move as Easy as Possible After Your Guaranteed Cash Offer.*

- Even MORE peace of mind around accepting your *Guaranteed Cash Offer* and moving on to your next phase of life!

WE WANT TO HEAR FROM YOU!

DID YOU HAVE a great experience reading this book? Because your feedback is so important to us, I'm inviting you to complete a quick survey about how you felt after reading it.

Simply call now:

1-855-967-SOLD

(1 - 8 5 5 - 9 6 7 - 7 6 5 3)

Or scan the QR code below.

SCAN NOW!

www.ingramcontent.com/pod-product-compliance
Lightning Source LLC
Chambersburg PA
CBHW071413210326
41597CB00020B/3481